DIVINE
FRIENDSHIP

REFLECTIONS FOR LENT

ANTHONY EGAN, SJ
TREVOR HUDSON
RUSSELL POLLITT, SJ

UPPER
ROOM BOOKS®
NASHVILLE

Cover design: Bruce Gore

Typesetting and interior design: PerfecType | Nashville, TN

ISBN (print): 978-0-8358-1796-7 | ISBN (mobi): 978-0-8358-1797-4 | ISBN (epub): 978-0-8358-1798-1

Printed in the United States of America

CONTENTS

ACKNOWLEDGMENTS

This book was made possible by the work of many hands. A special thanks to Margaret Backwell, who read the initial draft. Thank you to Margot Bertelsmann for agreeing, again, to edit the text for us.

The Jesuit Institute is also grateful to the staff of Mariannhill Mission Press for the work they have done. Thank you to Rob Riedlinger, the director of the press, for your enthusiasm on this and so many other projects we have embarked upon. In particular, we would like to say a big thank-you to Natalie Gallet for all that she has done to help in the production of this book.

Finally, the Jesuit Institute is grateful to Trevor Hudson, who agreed to be one of the writers of this book. Trevor preaches, teaches, and ministers in South Africa and internationally. We are grateful for his friendship. We are grateful for the witness of his life in Jesus Christ. You, Trevor, have enriched the lives of many people, and this book is just another way in which many will be blessed by your gentle spiritual wisdom.

INTRODUCTION

Lent is a graced time in the annual Christian calendar. The six weeks of Lent give Christians an opportunity to examine their lives and take their spiritual temperature, so to speak. Lent provides space for self-renewal. Most importantly, Lent is a time in which Christians are invited to deepen their friendship with God. Our efforts alone will not transform us. Only through a deep friendship with God can we be transformed. Friendship with God, in the person of Christ, changes everything about us. It affects the way we see ourselves, others, and the world around us. It changes what we most deeply desire. It gives us the grace to become the people God wants us to be: "fully human and fully alive," as the words ascribed to Saint Irenaeus tell us.

This book of Lenten reflections will help you develop a deeper friendship with God over the next six weeks. Use this resource to reflect on, grow, deepen, and rediscover the wonderful gift of friendship that God offers each of us in and through Christ Jesus. The reflections serve as springboards into dialogue with God. They are "trampolines" into prayer. Ultimately, they serve as a pathway into personal conversation with God, a conversation that will lead to a deep and enduring friendship. Set aside fifteen to twenty minutes every day (or longer if you can), find a quiet space to relax, and read the scripture texts and the daily meditation. We've included a few questions at the end of each meditation to help you apply what you've read to your own life. These questions can also be used for group discussions. We have incorporated the Easter Octave into the book. Many stories in the days between Easter Sunday and the Second Sunday of Easter are filled with wonderful accounts of the Resurrection and Christ's desire for friendship with us.

The daily scripture texts come from the Roman Catholic Lectionary. The lectionary offers three texts every weekday—one from the Old Testament, a psalm, and one Gospel text. On Sundays, the lectionary provides four texts— one from the Old Testament, a psalm, a text from the New Testament, and a

Gospel reading. The lectionary is arranged in a three-year cycle so that, over the course of those years, most of the scriptures will be read in public worship. Additionally, some lectionary texts are taken from the Apocrypha. If you are not familiar with the Apocrypha, some stories may be new to you.

This book contains the contributions of three writers. Their styles vary; some reflections use stories, some are based on personal experience, and others apply the daily scripture texts to what is going on in the world. Hopefully this diversity will also offer depth to your experience. May this Lent be, for you, one of challenge, growth, and an ever-deepening friendship with our Lord and Savior, Jesus Christ.

Ash Wednesday
A User's Guide

In the ash a sign,
In waters new hope.
Mix together. And
Apply on forehead.

Remember that you,
Remember that I
Are/am dust. Repent.
Believe the good news.

Each time it's the same
Yearly reminder;
Sign on the forehead,
Reminder to the soul.

Remember that I,
Remember that you
Am/are dust. Repent.
Believe the good news.

—Anthony Egan, SJ

Ash Wednesday

Read Joel 2:12-18; Psalm 51; 2 Corinthians 5:20–6:2;
Matthew 6:1-6, 16-18.

Lent is a time for renewing our friendship with God. In the busyness of our lives, our relationship with God can fray like the ends of a rope. Friendships can lose their momentum when we become engrossed in the grind of daily life and don't make time to hang out with friends. This can also happen in our relationship with God. During Lent, Jesus invites us into a renewed friendship. He invites us to "catch up" on the things that have happened in our lives that we have not told him about. Today, specifically, Jesus invites us to put God at the center of our lives. He knows that in doing so we will reclaim our true identity as beloved sons and daughters of a God who deeply desires friendship with us.

Notice how difficult this can be for us. Often, we focus on the external parts of our lives and trick ourselves into believing that others' perceptions of us matter a great deal. We desperately want others to notice us because we feel good or worthwhile when they do. We seek others' approval to feel validated and valued. In the Gospel reading today, Jesus reminds us that our true value is realized only in our friendship with God. God has created and gifted each of us, and, through friendship with God alone, our deepest yearnings will be satisfied.

The season of Lent—if we open ourselves to grace—can lead us into an ever-deepening relationship with God. Lent invites us to explore the attitudes, hurts, grudges, past situations, past relationships, addictions, and so on that have filled our lives and prevented us from deepening our relationship with God. Sometimes these things occupy valuable space in our lives and prevent us from moving forward. Jesus wants to help us bring them before God so that we can let them go and, in so doing, reenter the place of truth where we reclaim our identity.

The ashes that pastors distribute today remind us of our fragility and, paradoxically, our great value. God sent Jesus to live on this earth; God became one of us. The great mystery of God becoming one of us is God's way of showing us just how much God desires our friendship. We experience the life and love God offers us when we open our hearts to a friendship without pretense or secrets. This sacred time is an invitation to a renewed friendship with the God who loves us—no matter who we are, where we come from, or what we have done or failed to do. Let's embrace the season of Lent as a time to rekindle our relationship with God.

- In what ways has your friendship with God become "frayed"?
- What negative habits, beliefs, or insecurities occupy valuable space in your life?
- What will you need to let go of in order to put God at the center of your life?

Thursday after Ash Wednesday

Read Deuteronomy 30:15-20; Psalm 1;
Luke 9:22-25.

Deuteronomy puts a sobering choice before us: life or death? Moses tells the people of Israel what leads to life and what leads to death. We sense Moses' urgency when he declares to the Israelites, "You shall not live long" (Deut. 30:18), indicating that their attention is needed now. Moses describes the meaning of life: living in the love of God, obeying God's commandments, clinging to God, and dwelling in the Promised Land. Today, we find our Promised Land in a relationship of deep friendship with God. In the Gospel reading, that sense of urgency continues. Jesus invites us to take up our cross and follow him. Notice how Jesus invites us in the context of his own suffering. Right from the start, Jesus puts his cards on the table; there is no small print we can claim we did not see. He invites us to follow him but also warns us of the consequences for being his disciples: We may lose our very selves.

The call to discipleship is not easy. Following Jesus involves challenges. Discipleship is about renouncing what distracts us from giving God our full attention so that we can embrace more fully the life God offers us in and through Jesus. It is hard for people of faith to live the values of God's kingdom in a world where so much seems to be contrary to those values and, at times, even ridicules them. The world says, "Make a name for yourself! Be some-body! Why choose to befriend and follow a man who gets himself nailed to a cross? How does death display power and strength?" At first glance, Jesus' call to discipleship does not seem beneficial. But when we look closer, we realize that Jesus invites us to life in abundance—to love, happiness, obedience, and resurrection. We are not masochists, aiming to suffer and die; we are friends with a man who will lead us to all we deeply desire. And this life that Jesus calls us to may not be easy. But Jesus never promises us an easy life; he promises us the fullness of life.

Another way of looking at the call of the scripture readings today is to realize that Jesus invites us to get our priorities right. In the humdrum of daily life, our priorities can get out of sync. How easily do we become slaves (not disciples) of trends and what the world considers valuable? Lent reminds us of the most important choice we have to make: life or death? We choose life when we make a conscious, daily decision to follow Jesus, to make his vision our vision, to make his pattern of life our pattern of life. This means following him to the cross, but it also means rising with him to new life. The only way to abundant life is through friendship with Jesus and a convicted discipleship. Only we have the power to make the decision of "life or death" for ourselves.

- What does it look like to take up your cross and follow Jesus?
- What do you need to renounce in order to choose life?
- How can you make Jesus a priority in your life?

Friday after Ash Wednesday

Read Isaiah 58:1-9; Psalm 51;
Matthew 9:14-15.

Friendship is a two-way street; it requires give and take for each person in the relationship. In today's readings, the prophet Isaiah asks us to fast, and the psalmist implores God for pardon with prayer and supplication. But this fasting and prayer are useless without a focus or a reason for devotion. If we choose to fast—or give up a food or some other activity—during Lent, we do so to make a special place for God. The importance of our fasting lies not only in the physical action of renouncing something but also in the deeper sense and awareness of who we are making space for in our lives.

In addition to fasting, the prophet Isaiah lists other actions we can take—actions the prophet knows are important to God. Isaiah encourages us to notice the plight of the oppressed, the hungry, the homeless, and the naked. Our friend, God, cares deeply for these people—just as God cares deeply for us. If we can find a way of reaching out to those whom Isaiah lists, we will be doing the very work that builds a deep and enduring friendship with God. An awareness of the plight of others offers us perspective. When we notice the poor, homeless, or hungry, we are presented not only with an opportunity to reach out but also with an opportunity to thank God for what we have. How often do we spend our time wanting more and failing to appreciate what we already have? Our ability to exhibit gratitude does exactly what the prophet suggests: makes us people of integrity.

Our fasting, prayer, and awareness of those in need of food, shelter, and justice during Lent will lead us to a deeper awareness of God and of what is really important to us. It gives us a focus not only during Lent but also for our entire life. May we look past ourselves and focus on deepening our friendship with the Lord.

- How can you increase your awareness of those in need of food, shelter, clothing, and justice?
- What can you do to regain a sense of balance and focus this Lent?
- For what are you most grateful today?

Saturday after Ash Wednesday

Read Isaiah 58:9-14; Psalm 86;
Luke 5:27-32.

Jesus says to Levi, a tax collector, "Follow me." Levi leaves everything and follows Jesus immediately and then throws a party for him. The party gets tense when the Pharisees and their scribes question Jesus for spending time with "sinners." They know that Levi's life and profession are messy and, according to their standards, unclean. But this does not stop Jesus from wanting a relationship with Levi. Jesus knows that our lives are messy. He knows about the issues that drag us down and hold us back from becoming the kind of people God wants us to be. Even so, Jesus says to us, "Follow me," believing that we possess the gifts and potential to be his followers.

The prophet Isaiah reminds us of these gifts. We have the ability—and the duty—to help those around us who are oppressed, to be light in the darkness by our words and actions, to be like springs of water that never run dry. Since God gave us these gifts, God knows we are capable of using them. But what if, like Levi, we have been told that we are sinners and unclean? Perhaps we have found ourselves in situations where we made the wrong choice, where we failed to live out God's call for our lives. We may feel embarrassed by the things we have done, the experiences that we have lived through—some of our own making and some not—so we spend vast amounts of energy trying to keep the chaos of our lives hidden. We know that our lives aren't perfect, but we try to project an image of perfection anyway. This pretense and pretending can lead to deep sadness and isolation.

Today, Jesus reminds us that he wants a relationship with us even amid the mess of our lives. He sees our mess and still chooses to say, "Follow me." He does not come to call the virtuous but rather those with messy lives—people like us. We needn't wait until our lives are "perfect" to answer Jesus' call. He wants us to follow him as we are right now. Jesus will be our physician. All we need is the desire and willingness to respond as Levi did, and Jesus will lead us to a new life.

- What messiness in your life is holding you back from accepting Jesus' invitation to follow him?
- What God-given gifts do you possess that can be used to improve the lives of others?
- What do Jesus' words "Follow me" mean for you today?

Forty Days and Forty Nights

After forty days and forty nights
Satan filled with glee
Thought he had three bites—
Bread, power, and recognition.

And you resist
Because you insist
That to God alone belongs
Bread, power, and recognition.

Every day and every night,
O God, Satan tries to bite.

Give me courage to resist
Simply because you insist
That I belong to thee!

—Russell Pollitt, SJ

First Sunday of Lent

Read Deuteronomy 26:4-10; Psalm 91; Romans 10:8-13; Luke 4:1-13.

Let's be honest: We don't like to talk about our temptations. Very few people know us as tempted human beings. From the outside, our lives may seem free of any kind of inner conflict. The reality, as we know, is the complete opposite. All of us have evil thoughts, selfish ambitions, or dark passions that threaten to undermine our friendship with God and with one another. These experiences are part and parcel of our spiritual journey, yet we struggle to talk openly about them. But Jesus handles temptation in a different way. His own spiritual journey begins with the Spirit leading him into the desert to be tempted by the evil one. And we only know about these forty days of temptation in the wilderness because Jesus chooses to share his experiences with his closest friends. As a result, we know that our risen Savior was a tempted human being.

Jesus' experience in the wilderness reminds us that temptation is not a sin. Additionally, Jesus is not surprised or shocked by our temptations. However sinful they may seem to us, he knows how it feels to be tempted. Admitting our temptations to Jesus may be the most difficult part of our spiritual journey. We would rather see ourselves as virtuous and good, but this denial is not helpful to us in the long run. When we refuse to admit our temptations—our jealousy, our greed, our cowardice, and so on—our shame and guilt can cause us misery. Instead, let's share our temptations with Jesus—and perhaps also with a trusted friend, mentor, or counselor—so that he will provide us with the grace we need to overcome.

- What temptations are you facing today?
- Admit your temptations to Jesus and then listen. What do you hear Jesus saying to you?
- After you listen for Jesus' grace, pray the Jesus prayer: "Lord Jesus Christ, have mercy on me, a sinner."

Monday, First Week of Lent

Read Leviticus 19:11-18; Psalm 19;
Matthew 25:31-46.

In today's reading from Leviticus, we see two ways of expressing divine law. The first is through a set of prohibitions and the second a set of admonitions, but they can be summed up as the commandment to love our neighbor. In the essay "Two Concepts of Liberty," British political philosopher Isaiah Berlin divides the concept of freedom into two equally important parts: negative freedom ("freedom from" a range of social evils) and positive freedom ("freedom to" live a good life). Leviticus corresponds with Berlin's first category: God commands us not to steal, deceive, exploit, slander, or murder. In Matthew, Jesus' vision of the Last Judgment embraces what we should do to create a better life for ourselves and others: serving our neighbors, who include the refugee, the social outcast, and even those we loathe. We see an important progression in these scripture passages, as in Berlin's essay: The law takes us from what is prohibited by God to what God commands of us. Together, they give us an idea of the priorities of a faith-filled life.

Justice—to God, neighbor, *and* self—goes beyond simple rule-following. Rule-following is the bare minimum, a bit like obeying the basic rules of the road. If everyone were to do that, we'd all get home safely. But if we want to make driving less stressful, even pleasant, we must go further: We must change our attitude. Consider what would happen if we decided to be patient in a traffic jam. Getting angry is pointless. It also raises our blood pressure and puts us in a bad mood. What if everyone decided to be courteous to other drivers? Such behavior is not only good for others but also for ourselves; such courtesy will be shown to us too.

But what about those who take but don't give, those who expect to be cared for but don't care for others? Political philosophers call this the "freeloader problem." The laws, restrictions, prohibitions, and punishments in Leviticus exist for those who place themselves above others, those who cut themselves off from their community through their actions. However, if we live according to what Jesus calls us to do in Matthew—offering food and water to the hungry and thirsty, welcoming the stranger, clothing the naked, helping the sick, visiting the imprisoned—we recognize God in ourselves and in others and express the goodness and friendship God shows to all. By caring for others, we are affirming that everyone is worthy of care—even ourselves.

- Describe the difference between "freedom from" and "freedom to" in your own life.
- When have you found God in prison, in the lonely, in the poor, in the refugee, or in the stranger?
- What have you done for Christ? What are you doing for Christ? What will you do for him in the future?

Tuesday, First Week of Lent

Read Isaiah 55:10-11; Psalm 34;
Matthew 6:7-15.

One objection to prayer that I've heard goes something like this: "If God already knows what I am going to say before I say it, why pray?" It's a good question that deserves a thoughtful answer. After all, didn't Jesus say in our reading for today, "Your Father knows what you need before you ask him" (Matt. 6:8)? If Jesus' words are true, then God has no need for our prayer. Still, when someone asks me that question, this is how I respond: Prayer is not about giving information to God; it is about deepening our friendship with God. Here's a simple analogy. Let's say that I'm a parent. My child is involved in an accident and faces surgery. She is frightened of the upcoming operation and says to me, "Dad, I am really scared of the operation. Will you please pray for me?" Even if I already know that she is fearful, I don't say to her, "You don't have to tell me that. I know you are scared." To the contrary, I am profoundly moved as she shares her vulnerability with me.

Why I am so moved? I am moved because, in this moment of sharing, our intimacy is deepened. She is giving me personal access into her experience of fear and anxiety. She is opening herself to receive my love and care. Things now begin to happen in our relationship that otherwise may not have happened. We have a new depth of connection between us, a tender closeness, an experience of giving and receiving love. My daughter's willingness to share herself fills me with joy and affection. The experience of intimate friendship between the two of us is deepened.

This is precisely what happens between us and God when we honestly share ourselves in prayer. Through prayer, we enter more consciously into the rich, full, and free intimacy that Jesus shares with *Abba*. Through our conversational transparency with God, we open ourselves to receive more of God's mercy in the broken spaces of our hearts and minds. We give God's presence greater and more intimate access to our lives. Today, let us enter into more conversational prayer with God. We needn't put on a religious performance with fancy words and phrases. We can pray simply and honestly, using everyday words to share with God what is going on in our lives. After all, we are talking with the God whose desire for friendship with us goes beyond our wildest imagining.

- How have you viewed prayer in the past? Were you more concerned with sharing information or intimacy with God?
- Share with God, using simple words, how you are feeling at the moment.
- How do you feel God responding when you share the deepest feelings of your heart?

Wednesday, First Week of Lent

Read Jonah 3:1-10; Psalm 51;
Luke 11:29-32.

Many biblical scholars who study the historical figure of Jesus call him an *apocalyptic prophet*. This complicated term needs explaining. An *apocalyptic prophet* is a figure who proclaims a time when God's vision or judgment will be revealed. Quite often, this prophet understands that time to be his or her "now," and, frequently, the divine judgment he or she pronounces on behalf of God is one of impending disaster.

Both Jesus and Jonah, to whom Jesus directly refers in today's readings, offer a vision of impending disaster for an "evil generation." They say that God has condemned the respective places in which they prophesy. Jonah warns against some undisclosed public immorality; Jesus maintains that the people's lack of faith in him will lead to their undoing. What are we to make of these dire warnings? From the viewpoint of some biblical scholars, the book of Jonah is a work of fiction that illustrates how God calls us to prophethood and how we ought to obey God's will. Jonah, then, represents all of us—every one of us who resists God's call until circumstances make us listen. Jonah's story encourages us to accept our personal, God-given vocation and live it out, even if it means becoming unpopular in our community. In the case of Jesus' words in Luke, biblical scholars are divided as to the extent to which Jesus' pronouncements are his own or rather an interpretation by the Gospel writer of disputes between the early Christians and Jewish community at the time the Gospel was written. His words could also be interpreted as a warning to those having disputes within the Christian community itself.

Today's readings may seem to present a God who is angry; it doesn't seem like this God wants a friendship with us. But anger and friendship are not mutually exclusive. When we sin, God does not stop loving us—though our sin may anger God. This idea is, perhaps, quite difficult for us to understand.

Our human relationships offer us some insight. Parents, at times, may become quite angry with their children when they fight among themselves or when they disobey. Sometime parents punish their children in an attempt to teach them a lesson or form them into adults who will take responsibility for their actions. Even though parents get angry and sanction their children, they still love them deeply. So too with God. The scriptures present us with a God who gets angry when injustice is perpetrated or when people are harmed by the selfish and egotistical actions of others. But God, like a parent, never stops loving wayward children. God's mercy and invitation to friendship always are extended to us because God is love before all else.

- What in society makes you angry? Does it make God angry?
- What actions make you angry at yourself?
- How do you reconcile God's dislike of sin and desire for friendship?

Thursday, First Week of Lent

Read Esther 14:1, 3-4, 11, 13-14; Psalm 138;
Matthew 7:7-12.

"Ask," Jesus says, "and it will be given you" (Matt. 7:7). In his teaching on prayer, Jesus constantly emphasizes the importance of asking. For example, almost every line in the Lord's Prayer expresses a request. In our Gospel reading for today, Jesus draws an analogy between human parents and our divine Parent. If we know how to give good gifts to our children, imperfect as we are, how much more does our heavenly Parent want to give us good gifts?

Asking lies at the heart of prayer. Our reluctance to do so surely puzzles and even saddens God. Of course, we can abuse this teaching by asking for silly indulgences or selfish gain. However, as Anglican scholar Tom Wright points out in *Matthew for Everyone, Part 1,* "For most of us, the problem is not that we are too eager to ask for wrong things. The problem is that we are not nearly eager enough to ask for the right things."

Asking for what we need does not guarantee we will get what we ask for. This is part of the mystery of having a relationship with God and seeking God's will for us. But always, through asking, we learn humility, discover our dependence on God and on others, and allow both God and others to show their care for us. By humbly asking God for what we need—and also by asking companions and mentors for help—our relationship becomes more honest, vulnerable, and intimate.

Some of us find asking for what we need to be difficult. As we grow up, we learn to hide our real needs to avoid seeming needy or weak. The world has taught us that we always must appear strong, in control, and self-sufficient. Lent challenges us to become aware of our need for God's grace and mercy in our lives. It invites us to see how needy we really are, to stop pretending that we have it all together, and to learn to ask for what we need. So, let us look to God—*Abba,* our heavenly Parent—who cares more for us than we could ever imagine.

Let us begin to share with God what is really going on in our lives. May we ask, seek, and knock for what we need and open ourselves to how God will respond.

- How do you feel about sharing your needs with God?
- What makes asking for help problematic for you?
- What grace do you most need from God in this moment?

Friday, First Week of Lent

Read Ezekiel 18:21-28; Psalm 130;
Matthew 5:21-26.

Today, we have two rather fierce readings. Both Ezekiel and Jesus offer dire consequences for sin. If anything, Jesus seems the fiercer of the two, warning against anger and insults. We can take these readings at face value, but a more helpful approach might be to read them as astute observations about human life. Murder is seldom the result of cool, rational thinking; more often than not, murder occurs as the result of rage. This rage may be directed at a person who has done harm or at someone who has taken part in a dispute that escalates to violence. Sometimes this rage is directed in a more general way—toward individuals or communities who have harmed us or denied us our real or perceived rights. With few exceptions, the root of murder is anger. This is precisely the point that Jesus makes in Matthew's Gospel. He warns his followers about the unintended escalation of conflicts that leads to hideous consequences.

Even so, these verses lead us to this question: Is anger ever justified? Of course it is. Jesus gets angry, as we see in other parts of scripture. God is often angry. I find myself angry at individuals and at society. Being angry is not necessarily a sin. Sometimes we exhibit a righteous anger at people and societies that do not live up to what is right. Being angry in these circumstances may be a good thing. This anger signals that we are alive and care about what is going on in the world. In these cases, we are angry because we care not only about what happens but also about the persons and forces that make things happen.

Sometimes we may find ourselves angry at God, who, in the face of heartbreaking circumstances, seems not to care, allowing humanity to make a mess of the world, giving tyrants free reign in society, and permitting terrible natural disasters to happen. From our vantage point as mere humans without all the answers, we may feel that God should do something, should intervene. *Where are you, God?* we cry. But in our anger, we've begun a kind of prayer that sounds an awful lot like many of the psalms of lament in the Bible. Instead of letting our anger escalate to acts of violence or irreparable destruction, let us turn instead to prayer.

- Who or what makes you angry?
- How have you acted out in anger in a way that you later regretted?
- How might the anger you feel at God become a kind of prayer?

Saturday, First Week of Lent

Read Deuteronomy 26:16-19; Psalm 119; Matthew 5:43-48.

Our image of God is important. It affects how we relate to God, how we relate to others, and how we relate to ourselves. Sadly, many of us have grown up with negative images of God that make us believe God has no interest in a relationship with us. Deep down we feel that God stands against us, is angry with us, or is disgusted with us. Often, we fall into the trap of thinking that God is for certain groups of people and against others. We look at people we don't like and assume that God must dislike them as well.

In our Gospel reading today, Jesus presents us with a radical image of God, using imagery from nature. Jesus explains that God does not favor some with sunshine and rain and grant others darkness and drought, depending on their righteousness. Yet conventional thinking often creates the impression that only some are in God's favor and others not. Such thinking usually uses categories like wealth, gender, sexual preference, race, nationality, religion, and health to determine who are blessed and who are cursed, who are accepted and who are rejected. Jesus' image of God's all-inclusive parental care powerfully undermines this kind of thinking.

If we want our lives to reflect God's all-encompassing mercy, we must acknowledge our enemies and our actions toward them. If our actions have displayed a lack of kindness or understanding, we must admit wrongdoings. If our words and actions have displayed anger or hatred, we must consider how we can act out of mercy and love. For all of us, deepening our capacity to love our enemies is a lifelong journey. But as New Testament scholar Walter Wink points out, this passage in Matthew presents good news for us too. We would like to see ourselves as "just" and "good," but we are a mixture of just and unjust, good and evil. If God were not compassionate toward both the just and the unjust, the good and the evil, we would be lost. And if God shows compassion toward us despite our mixture of light and darkness, then God must treat our enemies the same. This good news encourages us to acknowledge our shadow selves, our tendencies towards evil and deception, and to bring these into our friendship with God.

- How does Jesus' image of God challenge your image?
- Consider someone you do not like and remind yourself that he or she is deeply loved by God. How does this change your view of him or her?
- In what practical ways can you develop your capacity to love your enemies?

So You Want to Sit at My Right

So you want to sit at my right,
sit at my left,
as crown princes of the kingdom?

Have you not heard anything?
It does not work like that.

There are no crown princes,
no crowns for that matter—
but a crown of thorns . . . never mind,
you'll get my allusion later.

Yes, of course you'll get a seat at my table
(unless you choose to sneak away for thirty silver pieces;
then, you choose not to be at my table).
No, not that table, the one in Jerusalem,
and, no, I've got no seating plan for that.
That one's going to be improvised,
whatever table, whatever room
we can borrow.

In the kingdom?
No, you miss the point.
The kingdom is a
work in progress.

—Anthony Egan, SJ

Second Sunday of Lent

Read Genesis 15:5-12, 17-18; Psalm 27;
Philippians 3:17-4:1; Luke 9:28-36.

The language of God's covenant looms large in today's readings. God makes a covenant with Abram, promising him and his descendants life, bounty, and, above all, God's protection. These promises are echoed in Luke's account of the Transfiguration. By appearing to Peter, James, and John with Moses and Elijah, Jesus becomes both the continuation of God's ancient covenant with Israel and an expression of the new, expanded covenant—with all of humanity. In both cases, the covenant God makes is dramatically different from normal, political covenants because it is a covenant of peace and friendship.

Political covenants, peace treaties, and pacts are made—in ancient times as now—between unequal partners. A powerful state or empire can enter into an agreement with a weaker nation, often making it a semi-autonomous part of its "sphere of influence." Protection of the weaker party is promised in return for loyalty and, more often than not, taxes. The weaker state often must agree to provide military support to the imperial power, to embrace the dominant power's culture, and to abide by its laws. Breaking this covenant is dire, inviting invasion, punishment, and, sometimes, enslavement. Smaller states have no choice in these matters. They must either accept the terms of the dominant party or invite mass extermination. We adequately describe such treaties by calling them *covenants of fear*.

God's covenant with Israel is similar but different in incredibly important ways. While God is indeed the dominant partner in the relationship with Abram (renamed *Abraham*—a sign of God's favor bestowed upon him) and Israel, God does not directly intervene to destroy Israel when it strays. Rather, God gives Israel the law (symbolized in today's Gospel reading by Moses) and the prophets (symbolized by Elijah) to call them back to their covenant. And through Jesus, shown standing amid the law and the prophet, we see the covenant extended to everyone.

With the new covenant ushered in through Jesus, we see his followers reacting in both awe and fear and Jesus responding out of love. Jesus does not condemn Peter, James, and John for their rather naïve proposal to build shrines for Moses and Elijah but sends them back to "the world" to continue his mission, which shall be theirs too. He warns them not to speak of what they've seen—this renewed covenant they have witnessed is something that must be revealed over time so that new disciples can receive it with joy instead of fear. Jesus wants his followers to recognize the new covenant as an invitation to love God, neighbor, and self—a covenant of true friendship.

In our own lives, we understand the difference between relationships based on fear and relationships built on love and friendship. Relationships built on fear allow the more powerful member of the relationship to take advantage of the weaker member. At its most brutal, the basis of such covenants is rooted in fear of violence. We see this in legal systems based on retributive justice, economies based on corruption, and interpersonal relationships based on abuse and manipulation. Whenever we abide by laws out of fear of punishment (rather than out of acceptance of the reasonableness of the law), pay bribes because there is no other way to get things done, or continue in a sick relationship out of fear of violence, we are party to such unhealthy covenants.

God's covenant that we encounter in Jesus is not a cosmic mirror of such unhealthy treaties. It is a covenant of love from a man willing to die for us, an invitation—not a command carrying threats of savage retribution—to friendship with the God we see in Jesus Christ.

- When have you found yourself in a relationship built on fear instead of love?
- What kind of covenant do you have with God?
- How has Jesus transformed your life with his new covenant?

Monday, Second Week of Lent

Read Daniel 9:4-10; Psalm 79;
Luke 6:36-38.

People throughout the world from all backgrounds and religious affiliations have been touched deeply by the compassionate leadership of Pope Francis. One reason for this has been his emphasis on mercy. Ever since his election, the word *mercy* has dominated his teachings and preaching. As he repeatedly stresses, having been embraced by God's mercy, we are called to become joyful missionaries of this divine mercy. When the church is faithful to its vocation, it extends mercy to all.

Certainly, this emphasis reflects the mercy described in the Gospels. In today's reading, Jesus invites us, "Be merciful, just as your Father is merciful" (Luke 6:36). Instead of offering us a dictionary definition of *mercy*, Jesus points us toward the mercy of our heavenly Parent. We are to be merciful just as our Father is merciful. Jesus knows we need an example of mercy to guide us rather than an abstract theory.

When I think of the mercy shown by our heavenly Parent, I immediately remember the parable of the prodigal son. This parable really should be called the parable of the merciful father. We know the story well. At the heart of that parable lies these words, "While [the prodigal son] was still far off, his father saw him and was filled with compassion; he ran and put his arms around him and kissed him" (Luke 15:20). Let's linger with these words for a moment. The whole being of the father—eyes, heart, feet, hands, and lips—is permeated by a rich, deep, and full mercy.

This illustration of a father's mercy invites us to consider two questions: First, will we open our hearts today to the divine mercy God offers? Even if we have not acted as recklessly as the prodigal son, we still stand in deep need of mercy. "Lord Jesus Christ, have mercy on me, a sinner" needs to be our daily prayer. Second, to whom can we extend mercy? Who stands in need of our mercy as much as we are in need of God's mercy? It may be our partner in marriage, a friend who hurt us, a colleague who betrayed us, or a child who disobeyed us. Today, we ask God to allow us to be the conduits of the divine mercy we have received. As we step into the cycle of receiving and giving mercy, following the whisperings of the Spirit, we step into the world of God's life-giving and transforming kingdom.

- When have you experienced mercy?
- How do you respond to the parable of the prodigal son?
- To whom can you extend mercy today?

Tuesday, Second Week of Lent

Read Isaiah 1:10, 16-20; Psalm 50; Matthew 23:1-12.

The nineteenth-century Russian anarchist Mikhail Bakunin was insightful when he warned against monarchs speaking of God, using religion to enforce their wills on people. We needn't be anarchists to agree with his sentiment. To see the truth in Bakunin's claim, we only need notice how politicians hijack religion to further their own ends or how religious leaders use their spiritual power to manipulate people. In today's readings, we see that Isaiah, the psalmist, and Jesus have anticipated Bakunin's warning by almost two millennia.

Isaiah points to the "rulers of Sodom and Gomorrah," symbols of unjust, corrupt rule and spiritual decadence, and denounces their violence and injustice. He calls them to repent, linking their actions earlier in the text to empty rituals and worship that lack substance because they are not accompanied by an ethic of care for the widow and orphan. The psalmist mocks such rituals savagely, just as Jesus denounces the double standards of religious authorities in his day. Jesus does not wish to destroy such worship and religious observance; instead, he points out how the establishment uses them to exercise power over others and make themselves feel righteous. For Jesus, God's law exists for people—not people for the law. And those whom God has called to lead us, in religion and society, are called to lead through service.

Between the call and the action, the law and what it stands for, yawns an abyss, a great gap that can only be crossed if those who lead us adopt an attitude of humility. Rituals of the law hold importance, but without love, they are empty. This is true for worship as well, where so often an obsession with the details clouds its primary purpose: praising God—not ourselves. Following Jesus's greatest commandment—loving the Lord with all our heart, soul, and mind and loving our neighbor as ourselves—ought to lead us into acting as friends of God and others.

Let us not be mistaken. Jesus, Isaiah, and the psalmist are not rejecting religion, ritual, and ethics. Far from it. In all likelihood, Jesus himself was a Pharisee—or closest to it in his religious background. His critique in today's Gospel is one of an insider. Apparently, he was not alone in this critique. Many Pharisees of his time were deeply concerned that extremists in their movement were confusing the intention of the law with the letter of the law. For ourselves, we should ask if our religious practices and moral traditions are advancing our friendship with God and with one another.

- When, if ever, have you found yourself hiding behind your religious traditions?
- How can you practice humility?
- How can you serve your brothers and sisters in Christ?

Wednesday, Second Week of Lent

Read Jeremiah 18:18-20; Psalm 31; Matthew 20:20-28.

Many of us struggle with the idea that Jesus came among us not to be served but to serve and to give his life for many. One of the main reasons we struggle is that if this was the way he lived, then as his disciples and friends, we need to live this way as well. Certainly, Jesus wants his disciples (and us) to understand this way of life when he responds to the mother of the sons of Zebedee, who asks that her sons be given the honor of sitting on Jesus' right and left in the kingdom.

In this passage, Jesus does not criticize the desires of his disciples to become great. He seems to understand their deep human need to live significant lives. Instead, he turns the concept of greatness upside down. Referring to the rulers of the Gentiles who lord their power over others, he says to his disciples, "It will not be so among you; but whoever wishes to be great among you must be your servant, and whoever wishes to be first among you must be your slave" (Matt. 20:26-27). We achieve true greatness and significance by giving ourselves for others. So how can we better serve and live for others? To live in genuine friendship with God is to become truly other-centered. Jesus' example must become our example—not merely because we want to imitate him but because his way of life is the highest, the best, and the most fulfilling. Wanting to be served by others is not life-giving but soul-destroying. Jesus reveals this to us. He is truly great because he lives to serve.

Our journey into service is nurtured with small steps. We can practice putting the needs of others, especially those close to us, before our own. We can offer to do some menial job at home without been asked, like taking out the trash or doing the dishes. We can ask a colleague at work if he or she needs help. If we only look around, we will see endless possibilities for service that inspire our creativity and imagination—and, perhaps, ask us to step outside our comfort zones.

Moreover, the Gospel invitation is not just about doing servant-like things; it is about becoming a servant like Jesus. This transformation takes place in our hearts and minds as we root them deeply in God's love and goodness. Within this divine friendship, we find the necessary strength and nourishment to give our lives away like Jesus did. And, when we do, we will discover a wild joy that can be found nowhere else.

- How do you respond to Jesus' servant heart? With fear? reservation? excitement?
- What makes serving others difficult for you?
- Name three ways you can act as a servant toward others this week.

Thursday, Second Week of Lent

Read Jeremiah 17:5-10; Psalm 1;
Luke 16:19-31.

In the parable of the rich man and Lazarus in today's Gospel, attachment to one thing leads to a disregard for another. The anonymous rich man (an inversion of the real world where the powerful have names and the poor remain nameless) has such great attachment to status that he simply does not see Lazarus at the gate. The parable is shocking for many reasons. First, we see the impossibility of the rich man's redemption. Second, we learn how negative attachments can lead us to ignore what we are called to do as Christians. The rich man is so attached to his wealth that he cannot hear the message about charity that permeates Mosaic law and the words of the prophets. His love of money has immunized him from experiencing true love. We see this in the obsessions people have with the pursuit of money, celebrity, sex, and power; in the captains of industry who seize leadership and pursue policies that benefit themselves; and in the demagogues who trash their countries and impoverish their people.

Some become so caught up in their professions that they lose sight of friendship with God and neighbor. They are too busy to see beyond their perceived needs. They rationalize that what they are doing is good for others—job creation, giving their children opportunities, providing security in an economically unstable world. These claims have merit, but do these industrious people in their concern for "others" actually see the concrete other, the people in need—Lazarus, for example?

Even in our search for greater union with God, we may find ourselves drifting away from God. By single-mindedly seeking God's friendship, we may lose our sense of God's friendship. We see committed Christians who spend their waking hours doing "churchy" things in order to prove their piety and devotion. Their perceived "holiness" can blind them to the real needs of others. But Jesus' parable begs us to get a sense of perspective. Before we

41

drift into our isolated worlds—be they political, economic, hedonistic, or even holy—let's ask ourselves the following questions: Does this thing we love and pursue fulfill the call of the law and the prophets to love God, neighbor, and self? Does it lead us to deeper friendship with God through love of the other, or does it blind us to the beggar at our gate?

- Who is the "Lazarus" at your gate?
- What prevents you from noticing the "Lazarus" in your midst?
- How do you define *holiness*? Does your definition help you engage with the world around you, or is it a stumbling block to genuine outreach?

Friday, Second Week of Lent

Read Genesis 37:3-4, 12-13, 17-28;
Psalm 105; Matthew 21:33-46.

One way of understanding the parable in Matthew is to read it as if Jesus is telling the story of God and God's people. The vineyard owner is God; the vineyard is the world; the tenant farmers are humanity; the slaves are the earlier prophets, leading up to John the Baptist. The owner's son can only be Jesus himself. Now, let's read the parable again. It is a story of depth, power, and sorrow. It tells how Jesus comes to the world to offer humanity an opportunity for repentance. And it is the painful story of how humanity refuses the way of the Messiah and allows him to be killed. Jesus ends the story by asking if those listening to the parable have ever read Israel's great song of victory, which we find in Psalm 118:22-23: "The stone that the builders rejected has become the cornerstone. This is the LORD's doing; it is marvelous in our eyes." The son and the stone are the same. Jesus, who will be rejected by humanity, will become the cornerstone of Christianity. The son whom the farmers reject will be vindicated when the owner returns and gives the vineyard to someone else. Ultimately, Jesus, whom humanity rejects, will be vindicated by God.

Rather than point fingers at anyone else when we read this parable, we ought to place the spotlight on ourselves. Do we recognize ourselves in this parable? As people so far removed from the time of Jesus' life and death, we fool ourselves from seeing our own actions reflected in the parable. At times, we too have rejected the way of Jesus—by living selfishly, by failing to love our enemies, by seeking only to serve ourselves.

Let's ask ourselves some tough questions as we seek to follow Jesus fully: Are we willing give up self-centered ways of living that go against Jesus' teachings? Can we focus on loving others—even our enemies? Will we put the power of love before the love of power? Do we want to serve or to be served? Is our deepest intention the seeking of the greater glory of God? Are we faithful friends of Jesus? May we wrestle with questions like these instead of pointing fingers at others long ago. May we seek to be true disciples of Jesus.

- When you read Jesus' parables, how often do you imagine yourself in the story?
- What aspect of Jesus' teaching do you resist the most?
- How would you like to grow as a disciple of Jesus?

Saturday, Second Week of Lent

Read Micah 7:14-15, 18-20; Psalm 103;
Luke 15:1-3, 11-32.

Today we look at a passage from the prophet Micah. Some of us grew up with a fairly negative image of God, so much so that the theme in this book—friendship with God—may ring a little hollow. Perhaps we hold on to the presence of an angry, condemning God, who waits for us to make a mess of our lives. The Bible tells us that God does get angry, but what kind of anger does Micah talk about? An anger that is overcome by love.

Micah's insight is helpful. Though God is clearly merciful, God also sometimes becomes angry with us. And how can we blame God when we look at the world around us? Even so, God does not harbor anger forever because God delights in showing faithful love. It is not God's nature to be permanently angry or eternally condemning. God wills for loving union—which we call *friendship*—with us. No matter how great our sin, including our complicity in the sin around us in the world, God desires us more than any anger God feels because God sees the goodness in us before the sin. In short, we were made for friendship with God.

The parable of the prodigal son captures the essence of a loving and merciful God. Jesus, in telling this parable, not only assures us of just how outrageously lavish God's love and mercy are but also presents us with his image of God. This parable is probably one of the most powerful pictures of God that Jesus offers. In the story, the younger son asks for his inheritance while his father still lives, which, in that time, is akin to wishing his father dead. After receiving his payment, the son takes off. He squanders his father's hard-earned money and soon is left lonely and desperate. Not only does he lose his dignity but also his identity; he does what no good Jewish boy would ever do by coming into direct contact with pigs and eating their food. In desperation, he comes to his senses and decides to go home to his father, presenting himself as a servant and not a son. The father, we learn, has been longing for his son's return, and when he sees his son, he refuses to consider him a servant. No matter what the son has done, he can never lose his identity or his father's affections. His father embraces him, kisses him, and clothes him. He puts a ring on his finger, symbolizing the son's identity as a member of the family. The father throws a party because his son was lost and is found, was dead and is now alive.

This is exactly how God deals with us. God sees the good and the potential in all of us before anything sinful we might have done. We never lose our identity as children of God; we always belong to God. God's loving mercy and desire for friendship always will be offered to us, despite our waywardness. Our repentance opens the door to receiving God's love and gives us a sense of belonging.

- How is your righteous anger rooted in love and mercy?
- When do you act out of anger instead of acting out of love?
- When have you, like the prodigal son, experienced God's mercy, loving embrace, and deep sense of belonging to God?

The Nazareth Effect

The Lord's Spirit speaks
a word of warning to you:
You are not welcome . . .

Prophecy unfolds
like this scroll before your eyes:
You are not welcome . . .

God's reign approaches,
believe me because I am—
You are not welcome . . .

Here to preach good news,
though tough times are coming,
the Lord purifies us.

Purifying fire
comes to cleanse us of our sin.
You are not welcome!

Catch him, stone him, purge
him from town and memory!
I am not welcome.

—Anthony Egan, SJ

Third Sunday of Lent

Read Exodus 3:1-8, 13-15; Psalm 103;
1 Corinthians 10:1-6, 10-12; Luke 13:1-9.

We all have experienced what could be called a "burning bush" moment. These moments occur when we sense that God is seeking our attention, speaking to us, and calling us to participate in what God is doing in our midst. Burning bush moments change our lives and the lives of those around us. They draw us into a deep engagement with the living God, who is always active in our lives and in the lives of those who suffer. Tragically, we often miss these moments, therefore missing out on partnering with God in God's great work of liberation.

To help us think more about this, let's consider Moses' "burning bush" experience, found in the book of Exodus. This moment takes place during an ordinary working day. Moses is engaged in the family business. As a shepherd, he is looking after the sheep when suddenly a nearby bush begins to burn. Burning bush moments take place amid the mundane and the menial. They can happen in a conversation with a friend, during a normal work day, or upon hearing about a need on the news. A burning bush moment is any experience that burns with God's presence. They happen all around us.

Moses immediately turns to look at the bush, showing that he is willing to pay attention. Instead of ignoring it to tend to his flock, he turns aside to get a closer look at the bush that is burning but is not consumed by the flames. Moses' awareness leads to an encounter with the God who calls him by name. Moses' encounter should remind us of the importance of paying attention to the world around us. We must stop, look, and listen to what God may be doing and saying each day.

The God whom Moses encounters has a deep concern for those who suffer. "I have observed the misery of my people who are in Egypt; I have heard their cry on account of their taskmasters. Indeed, I know their sufferings, and I have come down to deliver them . . ." (Exod. 3:7-8). As Moses listens to

God's words, I imagine him wondering, *This is great, but why is God telling me this?* Moses encourages us to begin to wonder how God may be calling us to respond to the cries of those in pain around us. What "human cry" has our name written on it? We cannot take on all the pain and suffering in the world, but we can discern where specifically God wants us to respond.

- Name a "burning bush" moment from your life.
- How did you respond to that "burning bush" moment?
- What "human cry" in your community disturbs you most?

Monday, Third Week of Lent

Read 2 Kings 5:1-15; Psalm 42;
Luke 4:24-30.

We were created with a deep thirst, one that only a friendship with God can quench. The psalmist prays, "My soul thirsts for God, for the living God" (42:2), yet we don't always turn to God to quench our thirst. Instead, we believe that wealth, prestige, fancy gadgets, or fame will fulfill our deepest longings. We place our hope in these things to make us feel satisfied and secure. These attempts only offer short-term refreshment and lead us down paths that God did not intend for us. Today's reading from Second Kings illustrates this point.

Naaman, the powerful army commander who suffers from leprosy, does not believe that he can be healed by simply washing himself in the Jordan. Naaman is indignant and accuses the prophet Elisha of sending him on a wild-goose chase. It all sounds too easy. Luckily, Naaman's servant has a deeper insight into the way God works, and he reminds Naaman that if the prophet had asked him to do something more difficult, he would have complied. He convinces Naaman to try Elisha's suggestion. Naaman does, and his leprosy is healed.

Often, like Naaman, we don't believe that God can fulfill our deepest desires. We seek fulfillment in the grandiose. We feel indignant when others encourage us to give someone who has hurt us another chance, to forgive, to share something that we have, or to be compassionate. Those actions appear to be unlikely ways to quench our thirst. Our search to quench our thirst may lead us to dead ends: a desire for wealth, material goods, popularity, alcohol, or drugs. All these "thirst-quenchers" lack depth. The more we think we are satisfying ourselves, the less fulfilled we become. Being in a friendship with Jesus helps us see that our own thirst-quenching efforts are futile. If we want to be satisfied, life with Jesus is our only answer. Anything else will leave us feeling thirsty.

- What are you thirsting for at this moment?
- How has God worked in your life in simple ways?
- Write down a few ways that you have tried to quench your thirst. Talk to Jesus about them.

Tuesday, Third Week of Lent

Read Daniel 3:2, 11-20; Psalm 25;
Matthew 18:21-35.

The message at the end of the parable in Matthew seems harsh. Jesus tells a story to Peter with the message that those who do not forgive will be refused forgiveness. Surely, this message seems a bit out of sync with our understanding of a God who desires to forgive us. Have we not just previously celebrated God's extravagant mercy? Is it not possible for God to forgive us if we refuse to forgive those who have hurt us?

Biblical scholar and Anglican bishop Tom Wright explains that the New Testament speaks with one voice on the subject of forgiveness. Wright likens forgiveness to the air in our lungs. We only have room to inhale after we have exhaled the air in our lungs. Our hearts, like our lungs, are either open or closed. If they are open and willing to go on a journey of forgiving others, they also will be open to receive more of God's mercy and forgiveness. But if they are closed to offering forgiveness, they will also be closed to receiving forgiveness.

In South Africa, I have witnessed some extraordinary acts of forgiveness. I will never forget the testimony of a sixteen-year-old during the Truth and Reconciliation Commission. Her father had been involved in the liberation struggle. He was detained, never to be seen alive again. She wanted to know who had killed him so that she could learn to forgive the murderer. Forgiveness surely must be one of the hardest things human beings are asked to do. But as Jesus reminds Peter, there can be no limit to how we offer forgiveness to others, just as God's forgiveness has no limits. But how do we embark on this journey of forgiving the hard-to-forgive?

First, we acknowledge the difficulty of forgiveness. Often, our hurt is deep, and we need to find our own "wailing wall" where we can express our pain and anger. Then, we need to make a decision. Are we willing to go on a journey of forgiveness? Following our decision, we should examine our own lives to see where forgiveness could be offered to others. This kind of honest self-assessment will guide us on our forgiveness journey. If we know ourselves as people who are loved sinners, then we will want to bring this pardon to others. Finally, we need God's grace to help us. But we can be sure that as we embark on this journey, however haltingly, God's grace and mercy will begin to flow through us in surprising ways.

- Who are you struggling to forgive at the moment?
- Share the pain of your hurt with God. How does God respond?
- Ask God for the grace to begin a journey of forgiveness.

Wednesday, Third Week of Lent

Read Deuteronomy 4:1, 5-9; Psalm 147;
Matthew 5:17-19.

The word *law* has many connotations. When we hear this word, we often think of courts, restrictions, and policing. We may associate it with a list of dos and don'ts. But God's law is not like human law. It is in place not to restrict but to bring out the best in every human being.

Moses enthusiastically speaks to the people he shepherds about God's law and customs. Notice that each of the laws are not simply restrictions; each law carries a promise of wisdom and understanding. God's law leads us to a new way of seeing ourselves and those around us. It leads to freedom in the truest sense of the word. Greatness, Jesus says, comes from honoring the law of the Lord. But we are called not only to follow the law of the Lord ourselves but also to help others do the same. God desires that we assist and support one another as we move along our spiritual journeys. Moses encourages his people to practice the law, knowing that their wisdom and discernment will be seen and revered by other nations. Moses also practices the law, knowing that he would be speaking empty words if he does not model the love and service of the law for his people.

God's law completes us and brings us to our purpose. God's law shows us how we can truly live deep and meaningful lives. When we live by God's law, we not only move toward wholeness but also inspire others to do the same. The law of God reminds us who we are and who God invites us to become, all while inspiring others with our actions.

- What does it look like to follow God's law?
- How is your way of life an example and inspiration to others?
- Who inspires you to live a life of love and service?

Thursday, Third Week of Lent

Read Jeremiah 7:23-28; Psalm 95;
Luke 11:14-23.

As friends of God, we are thrust into an intense spiritual battle. This struggle engages us with the powers of evil. Interwoven into the fabric of human existence, these dark forces affect every aspect of the world that the Creator has made good: the visible and the invisible, the personal and the political, the individual and the institutional. The good news of our faith is that these destructive spiritual forces have been defeated decisively. No matter how painful or costly we find the present world, Christ has overcome the world—and with his help, we can too.

Overcoming evil is an essential part of Jesus' life. Not only does he conquer evil in the guise of personal temptation but also he constantly delivers men and women from malignant evil as it manifests itself in human suffering and pain. Jesus presents himself as the Servant-Messiah sent by God to shatter the strengths of evil. Much of his public ministry, as we witness in today's Gospel reading, involves pastoral encounters with those held captive by these dark forces.

Today we observe the response of those around Jesus as he ministers to someone who cannot speak. The crowds speculate that Jesus either is equipped with special power from God or is in league with the evil one. Some believe the latter, saying, "He casts out demons by Beelzebul, the ruler of the demons" (Luke 11:15). Jesus answers by pointing out a contradiction in that logic. If Satan is opposing his own, then he has lost the battle. Jesus invites his accusers to compare him with other Jewish exorcists. Were they too in league with the evil one? If not, why should he be?

Jesus then clarifies what is really happening. He does this work of deliverance "by the finger of God" (Luke 11:20), a phrase that would have been familiar to his hearers. (See Exodus 8:19.) Jesus' healing actions exhibit how God's compassionate kingdom triumphs over evil. Later, his death and resurrection will demonstrate decisively the power of self-giving love over evil. Admittedly, we may forget or have difficulty believing that the crucified and resurrected Christ holds the victory over evil. We see the evils of the world—rampant corruption, escalating violence against children and women, the increasing gap between rich and poor—and become overwhelmed and dismayed. Lent confronts us with a critical choice: Will we yield to cynicism, despair, and apathy, or will we recommit ourselves, in partnership with the risen Christ, to protest evil wherever we encounter it? Only by constantly celebrating the resurrection message that evil will not triumph are we energized to choose the latter.

- What strikes you most about the way Jesus faces evil?
- What evil do you face in your own life?
- Name one practical action you could take that would exemplify Christ's victory over evil.

Friday, Third Week of Lent

Read Hosea 14:1-9; Psalm 81;
Mark 12:28-34.

Jesuit paleontologist Pierre Teilhard de Chardin wrote that love is capable of uniting human beings in such a way as to complete or fulfill them, for love alone takes them and joins them by what is deepest in themselves. When love is genuine, it is not just a nice, fuzzy feeling. Rather, love unites, completes, and fulfills. The theme of love is central in the Gospel reading today; it is the greatest commandment. Jesus assures us that love brings us into the realm of God's presence. Where we find genuine love, we find God.

Love is not quantifiable. There is no way that we can measure levels of love or know what the right amount is. Often, we try to calculate how much we need to give and how much is owed to us. Sometimes we "love" others depending on their "worthiness" or according to how much we think they love us. God, however, invites us to another kind of love. God loves unconditionally and deeply.

We have an obscure idea of what love is, often molded and influenced by our social environment and cultural norms. Valentine's Day is an example. Flashy and expensive cards, gifts, and romantic dinners are held up as measuring sticks of love. Many people feel like they are under pressure to prove their love in these ways. But these are only outward signs. True love springs from our communion with God and our ability to mirror that unconditional love for others.

Love also has a cost. When we choose to love deeply, we take the risk of being deeply hurt by the ones we love. Our hearts can be torn open when we are betrayed by someone we love. Our hearts ache when someone chooses to leave a relationship that seemed so right. God knows that love has a cost. When we turn away from God, as Hosea points out, God feels that same pain and rejection. The people of Israel, to whom Hosea preaches, betray God, and God feels the heartache of loss. But God does not give up, knowing that deep love will transform them.

When we love God with all our heart, soul, mind, and strength, the transformative power of love offers us a new way of seeing ourselves and others. When God's love transforms us, we can do nothing else but love others as God loves. God's love draws us into the very heart of God. When we dwell in God's heart of love, we are intimately connected to others. Love brings about union and communion. Jesus, our friend, invites us to experience God's love during Lent. His life, death, and resurrection are concrete signs of God's unconditional love. When we learn how much we are loved, we, in turn, can love others well. Love brings completeness and fulfillment. Deep love reminds us that we are not far from the kingdom of God.

- When have you felt God's unconditional love for you?
- Identify times in your life when you have been hurt—when love has betrayed you or caused heartache. Share these moments with God in prayer.
- How can you love more deeply this Lent?

Saturday, Third Week of Lent

Read Hosea 6:1-6; Psalm 51;
Luke 18:9-14.

I tell you, this man went down to his home justified rather than the other; for all who exalt themselves will be humbled, but all who humble themselves will be exalted" (Luke 18:14). These words of Jesus come at the end of the parable he tells about two men praying in the temple. One man, a Pharisee, seeks to exalt himself by telling God about all his good qualities and thanking God that he is not like other sinners—or even like the tax collector in the temple with him. In contrast, the tax collector stands with downcast eyes, unwilling to look up to heaven, casting himself onto the great mercy of God and acknowledging his own sinfulness. Jesus reveals God's response: The tax collector—not the Pharisee—is vindicated by God.

We have much to ponder in this parable. First, we don't receive God's favor by trying to look good. We simply can be ourselves before God without role-playing. We needn't pretend to be who we aren't. Clinging to a virtuous, overinflated view of ourselves is perhaps one of our greatest vices. God meets us in the stark reality of our broken lives no matter who we are, what we have done, or where we are from. If we can show our true selves to God, then we will experience God's transforming grace and acceptance.

Second, Jesus tells this parable "to some who trusted in themselves that they were righteous and regarded others with contempt" (Luke 18:9). We see in this parable how self-righteousness always involves a lethal combination of contempt, comparison, and condemnation. This unholy trinity is not accidental. If we are honest with ourselves, we can see how they work together in our own lives. Rather than face the realities of our moral weaknesses, we find someone for whom we feel contempt. We then compare ourselves favorably to this person, condemning him or her and elevating ourselves. We tell ourselves we aren't as bad as he or she is.

Third, this parable invites us to throw ourselves into God's merciful embrace in an attitude of genuine humility. We must go beyond feeling sorry for the condition of our lives, turn toward God, and pray like the tax collector, "God, be merciful to me, a sinner!" Our focus is not so much on how sinful we are but on the amazing depths of God's love in Jesus Christ. In moments like this, we focus on the God of mercy, compassion, and forgiveness. Only a humble person will acknowledge his or her need for God's mercy, and God exalts the humble. For God says, "This is the one to whom I will look, to the humble and contrite in spirit, who trembles at my word" (Isa. 66:2).

- How are you tempted to pretend before God?
- What is your experience of "the unholy trinity"?
- Ask for the grace of genuine and true humility from God.

Blindness

Blindness has many faces:
The lack of sight, but greater
The lack of insight.
Keep the Word in sight,
Gain insight,
Recover your sight.

—Anthony Egan, SJ

Fourth Sunday of Lent

Read Joshua 5:9, 10-12; Psalm 34;
2 Corinthians 5:17-21; Luke 15:11-32.

Today's parable—the prodigal son—may be one of Jesus' most well-known. This story invites us all—saints or sinners, old or young—to see ourselves in the characters. The title does not do justice to the story since it only names one character. It makes us imagine ourselves as the delinquent son, called back to God after having strayed. Apart from the fact that his motive for a contrite return is at best ambiguous—is he really sorry or simply pragmatic?—it reduces the father and the older son to minor figures in the story. This reading of the story doesn't allow us to walk in their shoes, seeing ourselves as both kind, generous, loyal, and faithful (like the father) and also skeptical, cynical, and begrudging (like the older brother).

Even so, the wayward son represents us insofar as we reject grace—which we are always free to do—and choose a path far from what God wills for us. The most vicious aspect of our young runaway is not his loose living or spendthrift character but how he embarks upon it. Claiming his inheritance while his father is still alive is the equivalent of wishing his father dead. It is an act of radical rejection. In the context of this book, it is the conscious decision to turn his back on friendship with God.

The father, of course, symbolizes God, who loves without reservation even when rejected. By extension, he is an example to us of the love we should show to those who reject us. The friendship—the love—never ends. It waits in hope that the one doing the rejecting will return. And upon return, it sets no conditions—no reduced status—to the friendship that is restored. Notice too how the father does not question the motivation for the prodigal son's return. He assumes the best intentions and greets his son with joyful celebration. How many of us could do that? Our human nature, buffeted perhaps by the reality of sin and evil we encounter, tends to be suspicious. But the father demonstrates that we should try to assume the best in others. We should be led by the better angels of our nature—not by our suspicion. The father reminds us of the nature of God: ever-loving and ready to welcome us back into loving friendship.

And the older son? He also represents us. He is all of us who look with suspicion on sinners who have "seen the light" and have been welcomed back. He is the reservation we hold about the authenticity of another's repentance, the cynicism we have about criminals who profess to be rehabilitated, and the conditions religious institutions place on members who have strayed. We welcome them back out of "charity," out of a sense of duty, but often with skepticism and dislike. Ironically, the older son excludes himself from that fellowship, the welcome-home party, which is God's reign. In doing so, he withdraws from full friendship with God.

- How do you see yourself as the prodigal son?
- How do you see yourself as the older son?
- How might you grow further into the forgiving father?

Monday, Fourth Week of Lent

Read Micah 7:7-9; Psalm 27;
John 9:1-41.

One thing I do know, that though I was blind, now I see" (John 9:25). This firsthand testimony comes from a blind man after Jesus heals him. While the disciples wonder about who is responsible for the man's blindness, while the religious leaders argue about who actually healed him, and while the man's anxious parents try to come to terms with what has happened, the formerly blind man simply shares what he knows to be true through his personal encounter with Jesus.

Being a friend of Jesus and sharing how God has been active in our lives can be challenging. Other people sometimes try to interpret our experiences for us, usually so they can put us into a certain category or label us. Some of our friends and family even may make light of what has happened to us so they don't have to take us (or God) too seriously. In this story, we learn the importance of sticking to what we have experienced in our friendship with the living God. It may be costly, but it is always less costly than denying what God, in Jesus, has done for us.

So how can we describe the work of God, through Jesus, in our lives to others? Perhaps we could tell how God has brought light into our darkness, a light that changed, healed, and transformed us. Rabbis tell us a wonderful story about a teacher who asks his students about the dawning of true light: "When can you tell the day is breaking?" One student suggests it is when we look down the road and see an animal, and we have enough light to see whether it is a fox or a dog. "No," says the rabbi, "wrong answer." Another student answers, "When you look at fruit trees and have enough light to tell the difference between an apple and a pear tree." "No," says the rabbi, "wrong answer." Finally, the rabbi says, "Day breaks when you look at a man or a woman and know that he or she is your brother or your sister. Until you can do that, no matter what time of day it is, it is always night." The true light Christ brings is simply this: recognizing the person next to us as our brother or sister. This is what it means to truly see.

- How has God brought light for you?
- Where do you remain blind?
- Ask God to bring greater light to your eyes.

Tuesday, Fourth Week of Lent

Read Ezekiel 47:1-9, 12; Psalm 46;
John 5:1-16.

Water tells us something about the quality of life in a community. When we see a dry riverbed—an all too common sight in southern Africa these days—or a river or pond dark with pollution, we may feel saddened or dismayed. Dry rivers cause deep concern for those who depend on them for sustenance; they are a sign of a drought that puts all humans, animals, and plants at risk. The very sight of one suggests death.

Similarly, consider a dark, stagnant pond. When we look into water, we hope to see our reflection, but a polluted pond only shows us the impending darkness of extinction. When we visit places where the only drinkable water is purified or bottled water, we may experience a sense of unease. I was recently in an African city where I couldn't drink the tap water. Even though I was lucky to have bottled water to drink, I was still distressed. When a state can no longer provide safe tap water, it has abandoned its citizens and broken its covenant, splitting itself between privileged elites who can pay for purified water and everyone else who must take their chances with waterborne diseases.

The images of water in today's readings offer an alternative to such a grim vision. Ezekiel describes the river as God's gift to us of new life. The river is mighty, healing, and nourishing, a symbol of God's friendship with us—the opposite of the broken covenant of countries who cannot provide clean water for their citizens. Water also features in Jesus' miracle at the pool of Beth-zatha. The pool is a holy place of God's healing, and the sick man who can't reach it represents those of us who feel we are somehow just out of reach of God's love. In healing him, Jesus reminds us that however much we might imagine ourselves as cut off from God, God's love reaches out to us and calls us to "Stand up, take [our] mat and walk" (John 5:8). The healing waters of God's friendship come to us in Jesus even when we can't get to them ourselves.

- What makes you feel cut off from God's friendship?
- Who or what in your life provides you with a sense of nourishment and healing?
- Who might need your prayers to find healing—a family member or a friend? Pray for him or her today.

Wednesday, Fourth Week of Lent

Read Isaiah 49:8-15; Psalm 145;
John 5:17-30.

Sometimes we struggle to find adequate language to speak about our Divine Friend. Often the ways in which we refer to God are quite bland and superficial. Thankfully, by giving us some rich images and metaphors, the Psalms come to our rescue. If we read them thoughtfully, we will find our picture of God enriched, our faith nourished, and our lives empowered. They show us who God is and how God relates to us and the rest of creation.

"Great is the LORD, and greatly to be praised; his greatness is unsearchable" (Ps. 145:3). These words remind us that God is always greater—greater than our experience, greater than our tradition, greater than our theology, greater than our culture, greater than all we can think or imagine. One of the tragedies in the church today is how we trivialize God. We often make God small. But God is the boundless mystery in which we live and move and have our being. To acknowledge this about God is to be filled with awe, wonder, and praise.

"The LORD is gracious and merciful, slow to anger and abounding in steadfast love. The LORD is good to all, and his compassion is over all that he has made" (Ps. 145:8-9). These words describe God's radical goodness, profound compassion, and endless love, which surround every human being. When we feel discouraged, wondering if God is against us or wants to punish us, may we remember these words. This is the kind of God to whom we come in prayer and worship.

"Your kingdom is an everlasting kingdom, and your dominion endures throughout all generations" (Ps. 145:13). Perhaps the most persistent and striking image of God in the Psalms is the enthronement of God as King of the universe, the Lord over all, Yahweh. God's kingdom has existed for all eternity and will never end. It cannot be shaken (see Hebrews 12:27) or defeated. It is not something we manufacture or produce through our own efforts. Instead,

God invites us to be part of it, to extend it here and now on earth, and to celebrate it joyously in our worship.

Psalm 145 provides us with just a taste of the words we can use to describe and praise God. In reading other psalms, we can expand our vocabulary for addressing and conversing with our Divine Friend. When we can't find the words, we can go to the Psalms and be inspired by words that will help us grow the intimate kind of relationship that Jesus shared with his heavenly Parent.

- What phrase in Psalm 145 attracts you the most?
- How is your picture of God enriched by this psalm?
- What perspective on your friendship with God did you gain from reading Psalm 145?

Thursday, Fourth Week of Lent

Read Exodus 32:7-14; Psalm 106;
John 5:31-47.

Today's readings are about religious idolatry and how it threatens God's relationship with us. On one level, we can understand the Israelites' idolatry in the desert. They embrace the one God, whom Moses has revealed to them, despite coming from a culture of polytheism. Meaning "many gods," *polytheism* assumes that gods exist in fixed places and that the god or gods of a place should be honored even by travelers who have a different god back home. In all likelihood, the Israelites interpret their difficulties as the result of not honoring the god of where they are traveling. Since they don't know the name of the "god" they have dishonored, perhaps they try to do the next best thing: They create a god in their own likeness, hoping that the local god will understand and pardon their ignorance. It's a reasonable mistake, given their understanding of the world, but it damages—almost destroys—their covenant with God because they are blind to the nature of the universal God revealed to them by Moses.

Similarly, in the Gospel of John, Jesus challenges the false image the authorities have of him and, by extension, of God. Over the centuries, religious establishments have created a distorted image of God and interpreted the Christian tradition in such a way that the God they worship has become grim, legalistic, and distant. And they are blind to the vision of God in Jesus. Jesus' anger at them is a mirror of God's anger at the Israelites in the desert. They have taken a good and loving God and created someone else, a projection of their needs for authority, for order, for a king to rival the human kings of the Roman Empire.

All this may be natural and even unavoidable given the impossibility of any finite human conceiving of the nature of God. Even in scripture, scholars tell us, the many ways God is represented is a result of the limits authors have in interpreting God's revelation to them in words. We must strip away human interpretation to get to the real God who seeks a loving encounter with us. The false images people have of God are not ancient phenomena. The temptation to create a God in our own likeness continues. The grim, legalistic, and distant God-image we see Jesus fighting against is still with us. We must work closely through prayer and discernment to strip away the layers that separate us from the true and loving God.

- Describe your false image of God.
- Where did this image come from?
- How can you work to discern the real God, the Friend of humanity?

Friday, Fourth Week of Lent

Read Wisdom 2:1, 12-22; Psalms 34;
John 7:1-2, 10, 25-30.

There is little doubt, from what we learn in the Gospels, that Jesus' presence evokes different reactions from different people. In Jerusalem, the religious leaders have mixed feelings about what Jesus is doing and teaching. Some say he is possessed by a demon. Others wonder whether the authorities know that he is the Messiah. In the end, they decide that he cannot be the Messiah because they know where he comes from; whereas, when the Messiah comes, no one will know where he is from.

We can learn from the religious leaders' mistakes. They are so set in their ways of thinking about the past and the future that they miss the present truth right in front of them. We must be careful that our assumptions don't blind us to how God works in our midst. As James Fitzsimons, SJ, writes in his reflection on this passage in John, we constantly need to be set free from the shackles of our own thinking, especially the chains of our so-called realism, which hold that we should only believe what we can see and test in a laboratory. When will we realize that with God all things are possible?

Jesus responds to his detractors first by agreeing with them about where he has come from. He has come to Jerusalem from Galilee. We sense no hint of defensiveness from him. Then, instead of saying, "I come from God," he challenges them regarding their knowledge of God. He says, "I have not come on my own. But the one who sent me is true, and you do not know him" (John 7:28). Because they don't know God, they are getting Jesus wrong. And since they are choosing not to know and believe Jesus, they cannot know God. We come to know God by looking at Jesus. He reveals to us the heart, nature, and character of God. He shows us how God goes about working in this world. As Jesus himself says, "I know him, because I am from him, and he sent me" (John 7:29).

- How do we judge others because of our perceptions of where they are from?
- What assumptions blind us from seeing the work God is doing in the world?
- How can looking to Jesus reveal God's character?

Saturday, Fourth Week of Lent

Read Jeremiah 11:18-20; Psalm 7;
John 7:40-53.

Living out our friendship with God as disciples is not always easy. It sometimes invites opposition and hostility. Others may question our motivation or our character. In fact, in *The Cost of Discipleship*, Dietrich Bonhoeffer writes that when God calls a person to discipleship, it is a call to die. Those disciples who are called may experience anger at those who turn on them for doing what they believe God has called them to do. Let's look at two examples from today's readings.

Jeremiah's anger and pain are clear in today's first reading. Faced with opposition to his teaching and threats of violence and death, he calls upon God to exact vengeance on those who fight against him. I can identify with his anger—even as I recognize the greater call to love our enemies and pray for those who hurt us. But haven't we all found ourselves in a situation where we want to cry out to God about a situation or a group of people treating us unfairly—especially when we find ourselves doing what we believe God has called us to do?

Another example comes from the Gospel of John. The hostility toward Jesus is strong in today's Gospel. Those whose interests are threatened by Jesus' preaching pull out every stop to undermine him. The trot out every trick in the book—apart from a serious examination of his teaching—that we see used in political debates today. They question his origin and challenge his right to preach. When faced with the fact that the people approve of him, the elites dismiss them as unthinking. When one of the elite, Nicodemus, proposes that Jesus at least be given a fair hearing, he is accused of being a sympathizer and asked where his loyalties lie. This reaction is as old as human history—before and after Jesus. Discipleship, being "friends in the Lord," invites resistance and hostility.

So what can we learn from these two stories? They teach us that Christian life will not always be easy. They teach us that being a disciple of Christ will entail resistance and hostility—the same resistance and hostility that the prophets of old and Jesus had to face. These accounts remind us that believers are never promised an easy life.

Another lesson we might learn is that of faithfulness. Despite experiencing resistance and hostility, both the prophet Jeremiah and Jesus remain faithful to their callings, faithful to their identities, and faithful to their messages. Jeremiah and Jesus invite us to model their steadfast faith in God. Friendship with God asks us to accept opposition graciously and remain steadfast in faithfulness.

- When have you experienced opposition to your beliefs?
- When have you opposed others' beliefs?
- How have you done your best to remain faithful despite opposition? What helped you remain faithful?

Before Abraham

Before Abraham, I am.
Before you lie in court, I am.
Before you throw that stone, I am.
Before you perjure yourself, I am.
Before you think you have the fullness of truth,
I AM.

I am telling the whole truth,
the whole truth because I am.
You'd like to catch me out,
make me villain of your drama.
You do not understand me,
I have no dispute with you.
But I can't be anything
But the one who says
I AM.

—Anthony Egan, SJ

Fifth Sunday of Lent

Read Isaiah 43:16-21; Psalm 126;
Philippians 3:8-14; John 8:1-11.

What we want powerfully shapes the way we live every day. No doubt this is one reason why Saint Ignatius paid so much attention to the transformation of our desires. He knew from his own experience how much they shape, in both good and bad ways, the direction of our lives. So let's consider this statement and finish it in our minds: "I want to . . ." In his letter to the Philippians, Paul writes, "I want to know Christ and the power of his resurrection and the sharing of his sufferings by becoming like him in his death" (Phil. 3:10). To grasp the magnitude of his statement, we must remember that he is writing from a prison cell. What he longs for most deeply, within the painful situation of imprisonment, is for a firsthand interaction with the living Christ. This is the most compelling objective of his life. He knows that he has by no means arrived; he wants to know Christ more in the mystery of his death and resurrection.

What does Paul mean when he expresses a desire to "know Christ"? There are two kinds of knowing. First, we can know about something through description. This is to know something at a distance. However, knowing something in this way does not mean we really know it. This kind of knowing does not usually affect us that deeply. Second, we also come to know something through acquaintance. This knowing happens through interactive relationship with whatever it is we want to know. This is the kind of knowing that Paul is after.

So how do we interact in this way with Christ? One of the best ways is to keep company with him in the Gospels. Perhaps we can begin reading slowly through one of the Gospels, staying in each story and parable for a few days, imagining ourselves interacting with Jesus, watching him, speaking with him, and listening to him. As we do this, we can follow the counsel that Saint Ignatius gives in the *Spiritual Exercises*. While reading the Gospels and imagining ourselves living them, we can ask for the grace to know Christ better so that we may love him more and follow him more closely. We can be sure that, as we do this on a regular basis, Jesus will step out of the Gospels, deepening and transforming our friendship with him.

Our deepest need, whatever situation we may find ourselves in right at this moment, is to live in intimate interaction with Christ. Therefore, let us ask the Holy Spirit that we may come to share Paul's desire to know Christ, to experience the power of his resurrection, and to share in his sufferings. In this way, we will come to live in deepening friendship with the living Lord.

- What are the dominant desires of your heart right now?
- How do you react to Paul's deepest desire?
- How important is knowing Christ for you?

Monday, Fifth Week of Lent

Read Susanna 1:1-9, 15-17, 19-30, 33-62;
Psalm 23; John 8:1-11.

No matter how wrong things go in our lives, God has the final say. In the reading from the book of Susanna, the elders and judges think they have plotted well. Then God intervenes in the most unlikely way and things get messy for them. The situation is reversed. The Pharisees in the Gospel today also think they have it all worked out and everything under control. Jesus intervenes and reverses the situation. The lesson for us today is that just when we think we have it all figured out, God may intervene, and our plans amount to nothing.

Let's contrast what happens in the two readings. Susanna is not given a chance to give her side of the story. She is brought before the authorities and condemned. Jesus, on the other hand, creates space for the woman in the Gospel of John. He asks her a question, then writes on the ground. He is in no hurry to accuse her or declare her guilty like the judges are itching to do. Jesus makes no judgment, only speaking words of encouragement: "Go your way, and from now on do not sin again" (John 8:11).

In Susanna's story, we see the harsh judgment of corrupt elders. Daniel knows they are lying before they even open their mouths. He pronounces judgment on their corrupt behavior. Jesus, like Daniel, sees the accused as a person with dignity. The elders see Susanna as a commodity. They cannot control their desperate aspirations to prove they are holier or better. They cannot control their own wayward desires. We do the same. At times we allow our wayward desires to blur our judgments. This can be at great cost to others and to ourselves—as the elders find out.

Jesus, our friend, serves as our model and inspiration. Notice how patiently he listens to others in their weakness. Jesus is slow to condemn and swift to offer mercy. Jesus sees us in our sin and offers us an opportunity for growth—and he wants us to do the same for others. This is easier said than done, however.

It is much easier to be impatient and judgmental; it is much harder to listen, understand, and be compassionate. But when we do take the time to do this, we give others the space to grow, and we touch the very heart of our listening, patient, compassionate, and loving God. When we are gentle with others we are reminded that we too are fragile and prone to sin. When we set others free, like Daniel and Jesus do, we too are more likely to hear the freeing words, "Go your way, and from now on do not sin again" spoken to us.

- Consider a time when you were quick to form judgments and condemn yourself or others. How did that scenario play out?
- Consider a time when you were patient with yourself and others. How did that scenario play out?
- How can you turn moments of weakness into opportunities for growth for yourself and others?

Tuesday, Fifth Week of Lent

Read Numbers 21:4-9; Psalm 102;
John 8:21-30.

Loneliness affects all of us. We may experience the loneliness of leadership when the buck stops with us; the loneliness of despair and depression, which is often hard for others to understand; the loneliness of superficial relationships with those closest to us; the loneliness of decision-making moments; and, most painful of all, the loneliness of grief when we lose someone that we love through death, divorce, or betrayal.

Today's psalm is the cry of a lonely man to God. Tucked away in this psalm are some haunting sentences that give us a look inside the psalmist's own loneliness: "Do not hide your face from me in the day of my distress" (v. 2); "My heart is stricken and withered like grass" (v. 4); "I lie awake; I am like a lonely bird on the housetop" (v. 7); "My days are like an evening shadow; I wither away like grass" (v. 11). One of the special things about the Psalms is that they help us to know we not alone in our loneliness.

Notice how the psalmist relates to God in his loneliness. First, he prays the truth of his life before God. He comes to God just as he is: "Hear my prayer, O Lord; let my cry come to you. . . . Incline your ear to me; answer me speedily in the day when I call" (vv. 1-2). Prayer often begins right where we are as we share with God what is going on in our lives. This is how friendship with God deepens. In order for us to grow in our friendship with God, we must become open and transparent with God by sharing as honestly as we are able what we are going through.

Second, the psalmist reminds himself of who God is for him, finding comfort in God's strength and never-ending mercy: "You, O Lord, are enthroned forever; your name endures to all generations" (v. 12). "For the Lord will build up Zion; he will appear in glory. He will regard the prayer of the destitute, and will not despise their prayer" (vv. 16-17). "From heaven the Lord looked at the earth, to hear the groans of the prisoners" (vv. 19-20). "You are the same, and your years have no end" (v. 27). The psalmist praises God for being attentive, compassionate, and eternally present. Today, may we allow our loneliness to lead us into an intimate encounter with God, who is closer to us than we can imagine.

- How have you experienced loneliness?
- How honest are with God about your experience?
- How does God meet you in your loneliness?

Wednesday, Fifth Week of Lent

Read Daniel 3:14-20, 24-25, 28;
Daniel 3:29-34; John 8:31-42.

We all long for freedom. All around the world, people fight for freedom and against various forms of oppression—social, economic, and racial, to name a few. In the first reading from Daniel, we learn about how three people, Shadrach, Meshach, and Abednego, survive the prospect of a horrific death—being roasted alive. They experience true freedom in their ability to trust God totally.

This story is full of drama. The king stokes the fire to make it seven times hotter and calls the strongest men in his power to bind the trio. The king, we are told, is astonished to discover that his plans fail and that the three victims are walking around in the heart of the fire. The king displays the beginnings of a conversion as he himself proclaims, "Blessed be the God of Shadrach, Meshach, and Abednego" (Dan. 3:28). Trust and faith in God bring the three to true freedom.

In the Gospel, we read about a similar struggle. Some of Jesus' followers struggle to understand and believe what Jesus says. They ask Jesus questions but find it hard to trust him and have faith in him. Contrast this struggle with the faith of Shadrach, Meshach, and Abednego. Jesus' followers use Abraham as their excuse for their inability to trust and believe in him. Jesus points out that he is asking for the same thing Abraham asked of them: to trust in God even to the point of being willing to sacrifice his son. Jesus invites them to trust him, but he does not force them.

The challenge that Jesus offers to his followers is one that stands before us too. Can we trust Jesus and do what he asks us to do? Do we have the tenacity of Shadrach, Meshach, and Abednego? We find our true freedom in our ability to trust and remain faithful to God.

- Where in your life do you desire freedom?
- What does having faith and trusting in God look like in your life? How is your faith similar to that of Shadrach, Meshach, and Abednego?
- What is your biggest barrier to faith?

Thursday, Fifth Week of Lent

Read Genesis 17:3-9; Psalm 105;
John 8:51-59.

For most of us, death is not an easy subject to face or discuss. We may have questions about death, but we don't often talk about them—questions such as, What will death be like? Is it the end of our personal existence? What lies beyond? How can we face death with dignity and confidence? Will we recognize loved ones in heaven? The questions go on and on. In our Gospel reading, Jesus offers words that may be helpful. He says, "Whoever keeps my word will never see death" (John 8:51). What do Jesus' words mean for our lives today?

These words take us to the edge of mystery. Jesus' words echo other powerful statements that he makes about death. For example, Jesus tells his disciples, "Do not fear those who kill the body but cannot kill the soul" (Matt. 10:28). Later in the Gospel of John, before Jesus raises Lazarus from the dead, he states, "Those who believe in me, even though they die, will live, and everyone who lives and believes in me will never die" (11:25-26). Furthermore, Jesus makes a powerful statement during his crucifixion to the thief on the cross beside him: "Today you will be with me in Paradise" (Luke 23:43).

Jesus wants his followers to understand that those who live in reliance on his word and who know the experience of living in the reality of his kingdom will not be extinguished at death. Death, rather, transitions us into a fuller, richer, and deeper experience of God's kingdom. We will not be hurled into empty isolation. Instead, we will find ourselves living more intimately than ever before in friendship with God. For as Paul explains in his letter to the church in Rome, nothing in this life or in death can ever separate us from the love of God in Jesus Christ our Lord. (See Romans 8:38-39.)

Having a hope in Jesus and in our fate after death does not mean that we have unrealistic attitudes about suffering or that we do not experience deep grief when a loved one dies. We cry, weep, and grieve like everyone else. But it does mean we can face the reality of death with confidence that it is not the end. Death has been defeated by the risen Christ and the God he reveals. With Christ, in Christ, and through Christ, our lives will always be held safe in the loving embrace of God's friendship. Every time we celebrate the Eucharist, let us ask the Lord to deepen this confidence and hope in our lives.

- What does death mean to you?
- How does your hope in Christ change how you see death?
- How can you best prepare for a good death?

Friday, Fifth Week of Lent

Read Jeremiah 20:10-13; Psalm 18;
John 10:31-42.

Agreat deal of tension exists in the scripture readings today. Jeremiah and
Jesus face the same fate—immense opposition—and both know that
their opponents have murderous intent. They place their trust in God, and,
even amid fear of death, Jeremiah sings praises to Yahweh. In the Gospel reading, Jesus tries, as he has attempted to do in the texts we have reflected on this
week, to explain who he is to those who want to harm him or disprove his
identity. Jesus calmly explains that if his witness is not proof enough then they
should look at the works he has done. These, he says, reveal that he is from
God. But, sadly, those who surround him are stubborn and have made up their
minds. In the opening lines of the text, we read that they already intend to kill
him. Toward the end of today's encounter, they want to arrest him.

The tension and drama of belief is also the story of our lives. We too identify with the struggle of the people who question Jesus. At times, we believe
that Jesus is who he says he is, and, at other times, we struggle to trust and
believe in him. Sometimes we are tempted to doubt when things happen to us
that are difficult to comprehend. When tragedy strikes our lives or the lives of
those around us, God may feel distant, and we may struggle to believe. Sometimes the notion of God may seem crazy. Often, the weakness and sin of others
in the Christian community leaves us feeling discouraged and cynical.

Over the past few weeks, we have been taking stock of our lives and evalu-
ating how we are living out our friendship with God by becoming aware of our
desires, our struggles, and the experiences that have either drawn us toward
or away from God. Hopefully, we have also discovered some gifts and seen
how our friendship with God has been (and is) growing. As Holy Week draws
nearer, let's now turn our attention to Jesus and the cost of being his friend.
Those around Jesus struggle to accept him and his new way of life. Today we

pray that we can believe ever more deeply in Jesus despite our struggles and that we may be loyal, faithful friends of his—no matter the cost.

- How do you sing praises to God even when God seems far away?
- Describe a moment of tension you experienced between belief and unbelief in your faith journey.
- What cost (if any) have you incurred because of your friendship with Jesus?

Saturday, Fifth Week of Lent

Read Ezekiel 37:21-28; Jeremiah 31:10-13;
John 11:45-57.

For two years, the religious leadership of Jesus' time has watched him, followed him, and spoken with him. But in the Gospel reading today, we notice a decisive turning point in their opposition. They hear news that he has raised Lazarus from the grave. His band of followers has continued to grow gradually. So they call an urgent meeting and ask, "What are we to do? This man is performing many signs. If we let him go on like this, everyone will believe in him, and the Romans will come and destroy both our holy place and our nation" (John 11:48).

Strikingly, this is the first time the Romans are mentioned in the Gospel narrative. The Roman Empire conquered most of the Middle East about a hundred years before Jesus' day. Though many Jewish citizens longed to be free from Roman authority and rule, they did not want the kind of violent confrontation with Roman troops that could end the religious and national life of their people. And they wrongly thought this would happen if Jesus' movement grew in popularity and strength. So they see this moment as an opportune time to make a decision to do away with Jesus. Only Caiaphas, a high priest, points out that they act out of self-interest—not altruism.

Now, before we throw stones at them, let us think of our tendencies to make decisions out of self-interest. Beginning in early childhood, we assume we are the center of the universe, hoping that the world will revolve around our wishes, desires, interests, and needs. The consequences of our selfishness reveal themselves all around us. Consider how self-interest prevents the giving of ourselves, sabotages intimate friendships, and ruins the life of the groups to which we belong. Reflect too on how the social consequences of this assumption work themselves out in the national evils of our time. They threaten to bankrupt the souls of our nations.

Could it be that self-interest lies at the heart of our opposition to the way of Christ? Even after we have committed ourselves to him, a deeply ingrained part of ourselves still wants to be in control, to call the shots. Perhaps we find ourselves in this battle on a daily basis. Camouflaged amid a variety of self-centered attitudes and behaviors, our self-interest continues to try to get the upper hand in our lives. Its disguises range from impatience in traffic, to withdrawal when we don't get our own way, to anger when we observe the success of others. But this Lent, let us return to our Divine Friend who never gives up on us, let us open our lives to his acceptance and mercy, and let us confess our failures and continue upon the Way. By following this path of ongoing conversion, we allow Christ to gradually transform our self-interested lives from the inside out.

- How does self-interest manifest itself in your life?
- How do you rationalize self-interest?
- Pray for an open heart that can look past your own desires.

Gethsemane

a darkened garden,
a soul burning,
sweat anticipates a crown of thorns;
friends sleep the sleep of the frightened.

a breeze or a brush
of angels' wings,
the cool promise of decision,
already a bit of resurrection.

—Anthony Egan, SJ

Palm Sunday

Read Matthew 21:1-11; Isaiah 50:4-7; Psalm 22;
Philippians 2:6-11; Matthew 26:14-27, 66.

Today we commemorate Jesus' entry into Jerusalem, and our readings reflect the light and shadow of the week to come: triumph to (apparent) tragedy, adulation to denunciation, promises of loyalty to acts of betrayal. Crowds welcome Jesus as their king. Another crowd calls on the Roman Empire to crucify him. In this we see heights and depths of friendship with God, a friendship that will be stretched almost to breaking point on Good Friday. In Isaiah, we see a prophet rejected, and we contrast that with a beautiful summary of Christ's life in Philippians—incarnation, death, resurrection, and exaltation.

But today let's focus on crowds. Research by historians and psychologists tells us that the anonymity of a crowd reduces inhibitions and allows people to throw caution to the wind, leading them to act out of instinct. Another theory suggests a crowd is more "reasonable," a coming together of like-minded people who draw strength from being together. Some theorists suggest that crowds create a new consciousness and new behavior. Above all, crowds create a social identity.

When we look at the rowdy crew who welcomes Jesus, what do we see? Jesus' followers gather openly, strengthened by their solidarity, joyously and uninhibitedly proclaiming his arrival, proclaiming his kingship. They create a group identity and draw strength from one another and from their expectation that something important is about to happen. It's Passover—a time of large crowds of believers descending upon Jerusalem for the festivities. The Romans dread this time because then, as now, crowds and common purposes can turn into insurrection, particularly amid religious fervor in an occupied country. They and their local administrators, regarded by many as collaborators and traitors, are on high alert. For a while, they can do nothing. Even Jesus seems to admit that. The crowd is unstoppable. So what happens? Why doesn't the crowd stay with Jesus and protect him—even when they see that he is not planning a revolt?

Arguably, precisely because of that. The revolution does not come. The ideas they have of Jesus are based on misunderstanding. The like-mindedness of the crowd is not the mind of Jesus. Perhaps Jesus sees the reign of God less as a national state than a state of mind—a mind that encourages everyone to live as if the reign of God has come. Perhaps Jesus sees the bigger picture, a new way of thinking and relating to God and one another, beyond the hierarchies that replace an old order after any revolution. If so, this is not what anyone expected. Disappointed, these previously welcoming followers disperse and leave Jesus vulnerable.

- What are your expectations as you cry out, "Hosanna"?
- How do you react when your expectations are not met?
- When have your expectations differed from Christ's expectations? Whose expectations will you follow?

Holy Monday

Read Isaiah 42:1-7; Psalm 27;
John 12:1-11.

Today we see God acting amid failure and adversity. Isaiah's sense of failure and rejection is contrasted by the promise God gives not only to sustain him in his mission but also to keep God's covenant with the people through him. In the Gospel of John, we see Jesus celebrating Mary's gesture of generosity and friendship, but beyond the walls of the house in Bethany the authorities are hatching plots to kill him. And even inside the home, Judas, who ironically is about to betray him, chastises Mary's actions. How often do we experience failure and adversity in our own lives?

Life is difficult, no matter how good we are or how excellent our intentions. Faith does not serve as a magic charm against suffering, sickness, and things going wrong. A close reading of the Wisdom Literature in the Hebrew scriptures reminds us of this fact. If we imagine faith in God will mean we'll be okay all the time, indeed that God just has to be asked and God will blow away our worries by magic, we're mistaken. No matter how holy we are, no matter how hard we try to do the right thing (and sometimes precisely because we do the right thing), bad things happen. What do we do in this circumstance—lose faith in God? Well, if we do, apart from having a wrong idea of God, we simply are playing the same game as Judas, who loses faith in Jesus and then betrays him.

We can learn from Isaiah. Instead of giving up on God and the mission to which he's been assigned by God, he complains bitterly to God. Nothing wrong with that. As Isaiah's friend, God does not do what we sometimes expect of our friends when we suffer—make it all better. Friends who try to do this often find they can't, and sometimes they make things worse for trying. Nor should we expect our friends to solve our problems for us. They are our problems; we have to deal with them. Instead, we can expect that our friends—and God, as Isaiah shows—won't abandon us.

Similarly, Mary acts as a true friend of Jesus in the passage from John. She does not try to dissuade him from his mission, nor does she try to take away whatever stresses Jesus may have as he contemplates his return to Jerusalem. She shows him kindness—in her case an expensive kindness, as Judas is quick to note. This attention she lavishes on Jesus is similar to the attention God shows to Isaiah. It is the attention of solidarity, without trying to fix the problem. It is the solidarity of friendship.

- How does God show up for you in times of trial?
- How can you change your mind-set from wanting God to fix your problems to appreciating God's presence during difficult times?
- How do you show solidarity to your friends when they are distressed?

Holy Tuesday

Read Isaiah 49:1-6; Psalm 71;
John 13:21-33, 36-38.

During Holy Week, the disciples' friendships with Jesus are sorely tested. Amid a meal, possibly the Passover or just before, two disciples profess their undying love and loyalty to Jesus; later, both will betray him. We too have experienced betrayal in our lives. Some betrayal comes from the deception of false friends—people who never acted as real friends but used us for personal gain. Other betrayal comes from what could be described as a crisis of faith. When faced with the discovery that a relationship was built on lies or deception—a friend is not who he or she claims to be or does not stand for the values and principles on which the relationship was built—we no longer have reason to trust the friendship. Is this what Jesus experiences in Judas's betrayal? Peter's betrayal of Jesus, on the other hand, may be more complex. Peter suffers a lack of courage. He is too afraid to stand up and be counted as a friend of Jesus, despite his bravado. He too is a familiar figure: the brave person whose courage deserts them, causing them to flee from dangerous situations, the believer who recants in the face of persecution.

In our relationship with God, the good news is that most betrayals—all betrayals, I believe—can be healed. In scripture, we see this healing in Peter, whose threefold denial is turned by Jesus into a threefold reaffirmation of love after the resurrection. Friendship at its best is unconditional. God's friendship is absolutely unconditional—an eternal offer that is God's very nature. We are always able to renew that friendship, no matter how far we've traveled away from God, no matter how long we've failed to communicate, no matter how we have betrayed God. Given that, I suspect that even Judas's relationship can be healed. He, like the rest of us, only needs to seek God's loving mercy.

- Who have you betrayed? What step must you take to renew and heal the relationship?
- How do you feel about the possibility that Judas is forgiven? What does that say to you about how you see God's friendship?
- What's the state of your friendship with God? How can you take steps to improve it?

Holy Wednesday

Read Isaiah 50:4-9; Psalm 69;
Matthew 26:14-25.

Today's reading in Isaiah emphasizes having courage in adversity. Courage is a virtue, according to the philosopher Aristotle in his *Nicomachean Ethics*. For him, as for his medieval Catholic interpreter Saint Thomas Aquinas, it is one of the greatest virtues. But great virtues like justice, courage, and moderation need to be applied carefully by appealing to yet another virtue: prudence. For Aristotle and for Aquinas, true virtue means attaining the right balance between extremes. At one extreme, courage can be stupidity or even a death wish, that is, taking chances and risking our lives for no good reason. The other extreme is cowardice, saving our skin and avoiding confrontation at all cost. Prudence, the exercise of wisdom to discern what needs to be done, gives us the ability to decide the right course of action when things are difficult and demand a response. Courage is not fearless, self-destructive bravado, nor is it running away from possible harm. It is the decision to act on our convictions in the face of opposition and threat, fully knowing the risks and accepting them despite real and justified fear.

This is the type of courage we see in Isaiah. He knows the risks of preaching and prophesying. He does not enjoy his suffering, but by the grace of his relationship with God, he willingly carries on. He knows that his actions are more important than his own comfort and safety. He makes tough decisions and lives with the consequences because he believes that his actions are of God and that God's friendship will sustain him in his trials. Isaiah's faith in God's friendship sustains him in adversity. Jesus' faith in his mission and his trust in his Father sustain him. Great figures who stand up for truth, including those strengthened by their faith, share courage in adversity. Thankfully, we may never be called to exhibit such courage. We probably will need only the courage to deal with smaller adversities, those things we sometimes call "daily life."

Even if we are not forced to face a supreme test, we can learn from the courage of Isaiah and Jesus and their relationships with God.

- What adversities test your courage? How do you discern what to do?
- How can you grow in courage and in faith?
- How can you share with others the courage you receive through your friendship with God?

Maundy Thursday

Read Exodus 12:1-8, 11-14; Psalm 116;
1 Corinthians 11:23-26; John 13:1-15.

Good leaders inspire those they lead through their words and deeds. Great leaders shatter illusions, giving those they lead a new vision as well. Good leaders appeal to sound reason, uniting people around common interests and goals. Great leaders further inspire love, the love that binds disparate people into a community of friendship that sees strength and unity in their diversity.

All too often, perhaps, when we recall on this day the Last Supper, a celebration reworked by Jesus from a meal during Passover, we meditate on the institution of the Eucharist by the words Jesus says over the bread and the cup. Earlier in the day on Maundy Thursday, at what the Catholic tradition calls the Chrism Mass, where the oils used for baptism, confirmation, holy orders, and the anointing of the sick are blessed by the bishop, there is also the celebration of the birth of the Christian ministerial priesthood, a specific development of the common priesthood of all baptized Christians. This Mass focuses on service rather than the Eucharist.

Most readers may find John an odd Gospel at the best of times. Here, for example, where the other Gospels focus on the bread and wine, the Gospel of John describes Jesus washing his disciples' feet. Judged from the standpoint of the first century, this act is quite scandalous. Washing feet and other menial tasks at table is the work of a servant or slave—not the leader of an emerging religion! The disciples are taken aback. Additionally, they are shocked and thoroughly disturbed by his proclamations, "This is my body. . . . This is my blood," recounted in the other Gospels. (See Matthew 26:26-28; Mark 14:22-24.) Peter resists Jesus' act of service. But Jesus shatters his illusions. He explains that leadership requires service. Leadership goes beyond skills in preaching, healing, exorcising demons, administering sacraments, and presiding over worship. A true leader serves the community.

Imagine almost any organization today. How does its leadership lead? In many corporations, I suspect the exact opposite of what Jesus requires of his disciples is going on. A board of directors and CEO give the orders. In the past they may have been quite distant, aloof, and unreachable, but now workers may know the names of those whose decisions affect their jobs. Middle management bosses the minions around, while often battling one another to get noticed for promotion. At the very bottom of the pile, we find the cleaning staff—the object of everyone's complaint, often invisible because they do their jobs at night when everyone is home.

And we can't deny that the same is true for our religious organizations. Anyone who's ever been involved in church leadership, education, or lay organizations can tell stories that are similar to those in business or politics. Similarly, among clergy and ministers of religion, we may find the constant scrabbling for favor, the jealous guarding of religious turf, and the pursuit of higher office. The religious world all too often mirrors the rest of the world.

All of this is the polar opposite of what Jesus intends. Those who lead should serve—and not in some pious, smarmy manner that is simply a strategy to become ingratiated to those in power. Genuine service calls for the giving of ourselves to others to build community and relationships. It is the process of building up friendship for the service of the world.

- Describe your own leadership strategy, whether at work, in the home, in a faith community, or in a civic organization.
- How do you combine leading with service?
- How is your leadership an expression of your faith?

Good Friday

Seven Last Words

Good Friday represents the climax of the drama of our salvation. It illustrates the extent to which God in Jesus of Nazareth is ready to show solidarity with humanity, a solidarity that saves us. Drawn from the four canonical Gospels, Jesus' words on the cross—often called the Seven Last Words or Seven Words—each highlight an aspect of our theme, friendship with God.

As he is crucified, Jesus proclaims, "Father, forgive them; for they do not know what they are doing" (Luke 23:34). Jesus' willingness to forgive is absolute, without condition. Throughout his life and by his words and deeds, he has forgiven sins. Now he forgives those who have shown him the ultimate rejection. Forgiving our enemies often is easier than forgiving our friends. We can keep our enemies at a distance. They do not impinge much on our consciousness. We can indeed forgive—and forget. With friends, the circumstances are different. Friends are always around. They are part of our circle. When a friend hurts me, even though I may forgive him, I do not easily forget his actions. I am one of those people who is "once bitten, twice shy." My trust is earned. Once lost, even by a close friend, it is not easily regained. I look upon a friend who has hurt me and often wonder whether she'll hurt me again. We must all pray for the grace to forgive as Jesus does.

During Jesus' crucifixion, he sees his mother standing next to his beloved disciples, and he says, "Woman, here is your son" (John 19:26). To his disciple, he says, "Here is your mother" (John 19:27). Even as he is dying, Jesus expresses God's friendship with us by creating a new community. The mark of friendship is community—we are the family of God. During times of crisis and suffering, we are to pull together, build new communities—new families—out of the remnants of the old. Those who work among refugees and forced migrants have told me how one of the greatest urges of displaced people is to rebuild community. A mark of God's friendship with us is God's desire to rebuild bonds that have been broken. New life and new relationships must emerge out of the ashes.

Amid the taunts from the soldiers and the crowd of scornful onlookers, one voice—a dying criminal—offers a different request. Acknowledging his crimes that have led to his execution, this anonymous figure asks Jesus to remember him. Jesus' reply, "Today you will be with me in Paradise" (Luke 23:43), is more than just consoling words. It is an expression of reconciliation, a reconnection of the thief with the beloved community. God's friendship extends even to those who by their actions have chosen to exclude themselves from God. The power of evil is ultimately a self-made illusion. Evil has power only insofar we let it. In rejecting our sin and reaching out to God, we discover God's friendship embracing us, drawing us back to our true selves and destiny, which is union with God.

Jesus' cry, "I am thirsty" (John 19:28), is not just a need for drink. On a deeper level, it is a yearning for connection, reconnection with the love that is friendship with God. We see this expressed in many places and times among those separated from loved ones by conflict, suffering, and death. I recall the restlessness and longing that marks the writings of imprisoned anti-Nazi activist Dietrich Bonhoeffer as he awaited execution. Our own thirst for connection is summed up by Saint Augustine's own restlessness until he rested in God.

Despair and hope coexist in Jesus' great cry, "My God, my God, why have you forsaken me?" (Mark 15:34). Read alone, it is despairing. Some scholars, like Jürgen Moltmann, himself traumatized as a conscript during the WWII, highlight the tension here between Father and Son, a tension that almost reaches breaking point. If we emphasize the "almost" over the "breaking point," I find this a useful insight. Suffering can make us wonder where God is, whether God really is our friend, indeed whether God even exists. Read in the context of its literary source (Psalm 22), however, it is a cry of anguish that is transformed into triumph. The sense of separation, abandonment by God, is transformed into a deep consolation that even in the midst of extreme suffering God has not turned away from us. It may be hard for us to see God's friendship, but it is there.

Just before Jesus' death on the cross, Luke's account records him saying, "Father, into your hands I commend my spirit" (23:46). Jesus surrenders himself completely into God's hands. This is not the first time we have seen Jesus surrendering to God; he does this in the garden of Gethsemane when he prays, "Not my will but yours be done" (Luke 22:42). In his last moments of life, Jesus teaches us that any deep and enduring friendship will have trust and surrender at its cornerstone. His trust and surrender at this moment will lead, ultimately, to resurrection.

As often happens in the Gospel of John, the final moments of the crucifixion differ from the other Gospels. Jesus' final words, "It is finished" (John 19:30), are a statement of triumph. Jesus has lived God's solidarity with us to the absolute limit—rejection and death. He has not broken faith with humanity. The bond of friendship between God and us remains intact.

- When have you felt abandoned by God?
- How can you transform your suffering into solidarity with Jesus and others?
- What keeps you believing that resurrection lies beyond suffering and death?

Holy Saturday

There are no scripture readings today. We invite you to live this day between death and life, to wait, to watch, and to hope in silence.

Pontius Pilate

The Galilean is dead. Potential disaster has been averted. His followers have scattered, and the Jews go about their annual Passover rituals. Thanks to my quick thinking, along with that of High Priest Caiaphas, his colleagues, and Herod, the Tetrarch of Galilee, the crisis initiated by the arrival of Jesus the Nazarene last week in this provincial town of Jerusalem (I will not call it a city, for Rome is the only real city on this earth) is over. There will be no rebellion under my watch.

Peter

He is dead. We are in hiding, all of us. From the roof of our safe house, I can see that accursed hill, Golgotha. Today, under a bleak sun—at least the sun seems bleak to me, when it does not scowl down on me in accusation—I can see the permanent wooden posts on which the crossbeams are hung during times of execution. They stick out more prominently today like ugly fingers pointing directly to the heavens, in defiance of God. Sometimes I think they point at me, at my cowardice.

Biblical Scholar

It was uncommon for crucified criminals, particularly those who rebelled against Rome, to receive a normal burial. After insurrections, like that in Palestine in 6 CE, thousands of rebels were crucified at regular intervals on the Roman roads, their bodies left to rot or be eaten by carrion (as had happened in Italy decades earlier during the slave revolt led by Spartacus).

Centurion

At least the decent one we executed was not thrown onto the dump like we did with the others, to rot in this accursed heat as wild dogs and vultures pick at them. I am not squeamish by nature—I have killed men in battle, executed many more, including many in this vile place. But somehow this man seemed different.

Mary Magdalene

I am devastated. He who cured me of my seven demons, whom I loved—love—is dead. How often I have listened to him tell his wonderful stories, filled with barbed wit that skewers the pious pretension and puffed up arrogance of the men who dominate us, who make us—women, daughters of Abraham—feel little more than sheep to be herded and traded by them. We—his mother, the other Mary (Lazarus's sister), and myself—who have traveled with him and his band of disciples, are shattered. It is all too much for his mother, though she says an angel once told her that a spear would pierce her heart. She sits with us weeping, staring out in the direction of that horrible place where yesterday we stood alone with young John, waiting for our beloved to die. Thank God for that kind man Joseph, who offered to bury him rather than leave him to the dogs and vultures.

Caiaphas

It's always a tragedy to see a man die, a son of Israel—however misguided he might be. It's no crime to be deluded, whatever we said yesterday morning. Of course, his comments were heretical, possibly blasphemous. Normally a good beating, then a spell in a cell, then a swift cart ride to the city gates, and a warning to stay out of this Holy City until he's regained his senses would suffice. But at this time, with Rome breathing down our necks—no, there was no choice. One man, as we noted, had to die for the people. For the people. For God's people. Our people.

Peter

You fool, Simon! You should have stuck to fishing. You are no good at this wandering around, let alone leading the Twelve. In his hour of deepest need, having just made absurd public protestations of love and loyalty unto death, you deny him! And then you hide here in this nasty little upper room. Big, brave, blustery Peter! This rock has cracked into pebbles under pressure. No, not pebbles, grains of dust. How could you have chosen me, Lord? How could you have asked me to lead them?

Mary Magdalene

To keep busy, to keep sane—my spirit is too low, my mind too distracted to pray even on this holy day—I have been collecting oils and ointments. I have told my sorrowful sisters that after sabbath tomorrow morning, early, before sunrise, I am going back to the tomb to anoint his body. It is the least I can do. He had no honorable burial. I shall give him that. They want to come with me. No doubt the men will remain in hiding until the city quiets down and they can go back home, those who haven't already slunk away into the night.

Peter

Just got news: Judas, the traitor, has been found. Hanged in a field. Thirty pieces of silver—his payoff no doubt—scattered around him. Suicide—the Romans, if they'd been tidying up loose ends, would have pocketed the money. Remorse—couldn't handle the guilt. After what he did, I should feel glee at his death. But after what I did, I think I understand him.

Pontius Pilate

Do I worry, as my wife does, about this Jesus of Nazareth fellow? Not a bit. He defied Rome, albeit in a way I've never seen before. He embarrassed his fellow Jews, well, those who work with us to preserve the peace, even though they hate us like the rest of the rabble. He got what was coming to him. His death leaves me cold.

- Which of these voices reflects where you are today?
- Which of these voices reflects where you would like to be?
- Reread the voices and then wait in silence.

Gone Fishing

Some friends went fishing, one morning, to forget
all that passed between them. No matter the weather
the atmosphere was chilly, for some had heard rumors,
others claimed visions, and others said it was all delusion.
However full the sea, they were unlucky; the nets were not
doing their job. Obscured by the sunrise, a figure called
out to them to try once more. With little else to do, they tried
again. From that day on, whenever they went fishing,
alone or together, at sea or on land, in cities or in villages,
they remembered his call to try once more.
With nothing else to do and a world to gain, they tried again.

—Anthony Egan, SJ

Easter Sunday

Read Acts 10:34-43; Psalm 118;
1 Corinthians 5:6-8; John 20:1-9, 18.

Suddenly, in the depth of Holy Saturday night, a light flickers into life, a light that grows brighter and shines in the darkness: the light of the Resurrection. In many churches throughout the world we begin, appropriately, outside as we light the Easter Candle, the candle of resurrection. At times, especially if there is wind or rain, this is no small effort. But the candle is lit, and, as we move into the church, the congregation's candles are lit from this one candle.

"Lumen Christi!"

"Deo gratias!"

As the silence of death is broken by that ancient chant of resurrection, the whole church is lit up. When the congregation extinguishes their candles, they put them out in a community bathed in light and filled with songs of joy. And in the days and weeks to come, we read time and again the multiple stories of resurrection.

This morning's account, which includes Mary Magdalene's encounter with her risen Lord, highlights something important. The Resurrection needs to be seen not just as a single event but as a process in which the disciples struggle to overcome their doubts and confusion, even after the tomb is found empty. It is a process where each disciple must overcome his or her doubts and personally experience the Risen Christ. Simon Peter sees the burial cloths; how he responds is unclear. The disciple whom Jesus loved (usually understood to be John, but for some biblical scholars a symbol of all of us, the believing church) sees and believes. Mary Magdalene's reaction is clear—sorrow and a sense of double loss because Jesus is dead and his body is missing. Not even two angels seem to help her; it is only her encounter with the Lord in the garden that brings her to faith in the Resurrection. From that moment onward, she is unstoppable in her proclamation. Defying conventions that held that women could not be witnesses, Mary Magdalene tells the disciples that Christ is risen. From reading the text, we are unsure whether they really believe her.

How like us! How often do we go through the whole Easter Vigil with a sense of distance, a kind of intellectual assertion of the process but without a deeply felt conviction that Christ is risen? Or we accept the Resurrection as an act of faith but truly wonder whether it makes a difference in our lives. Our lives are so filled with other worries that we cannot acknowledge that the Resurrection is the supreme expression of God's friendship with us, the promise of God's solidarity with the whole human race. I know this feeling all too well. It is good indeed that the church gives us Easter as a season rather than a day.

For a few, perhaps, the whole thing ends on Good Friday. I am not talking here about a sense of despair and failure, an inability to believe that resurrection is possible—though at times even the most committed Christian may feel this. No, I mean this in a different way. Once, only once, while meditating on Jesus' last words in John—"It is finished" (19:30)—I was filled with a sense that the Resurrection had already started. The rest of the weekend seemed like an anti-climax. That's why we need to see the Resurrection as a process rather than a single event. It is a series of moments that define us as Christians and remind us of God's friendship that breaks through sin and the stubbornness of our hearts, which have become hardened by the frequent ugliness we see in our world. It is not easy to believe in the "happy ending," much as we'd like to. We must stay open to the possibility that God's friendship is so great that it breaks through to us.

Just as the candles of each individual get lit from the Easter candle, so too do we as individuals encounter our personal resurrection. A little spark becomes a flame that bathes the darkness in light, a light that grows into the brightness of Easter.

- How have you struggled to find the risen Christ in your life?
- With which of the disciples do you most identify?
- Where have you found resurrection this Easter?

Monday Easter Octave

Read Acts 2:14, 22-23; Psalm 16;
Matthew 28:8-15.

Today's readings are filled with a newfound courage and boldness. In the Acts of the Apostles, Peter (who runs away when Jesus is arrested and later denies him) now boldly proclaims the resurrection of Jesus. We may smile as we read Peter speaking his truth: "This Jesus God raised up, and of that all of us are witnesses" (Acts 2:32). In the Gospel reading, we also meet courageous and bold women. They depart from the tomb with "fear and great joy" (Matt. 28:8) and run to tell the disciples what they have discovered. As they make their way, Jesus appears to them, and they "[take] hold of his feet, and [worship] him" (Matt. 28:9). Jesus asks them to tell his brothers to go to Galilee and wait for him because they will see him there. The women become the first messengers of the Resurrection, but they are also the first to have a personal encounter with the risen Christ.

In these days after Lent and our celebration of Jesus' passion and death, we are being invited into a new personal encounter with him. In this fresh encounter we too will find a new boldness and courage and a renewed energy to be messengers of his resurrection. These personal encounters help us reenergize and renew relationships and friendships. The Easter Octave is a time specially put aside so that we, like the various people in the Gospels, can encounter the risen Christ again and again.

Contrast the energetic "fear and great joy" of the women—and the boldness and courage of Peter—with the fear of the chief priests and the governor. While the news of the Resurrection spreads, they do all in their power to counter the news. Cash is handed over to ensure that soldiers proclaim the party line: "His disciples came by night and stole him away while we were asleep" (Matt. 28:13). There is a very different quality to the energetic and joyful "fear" of the women and the "fear" of keeping the governor out of trouble. The women are open to an encounter with Jesus. The religious leaders and civil authorities never allow themselves to have a personal encounter with Jesus.

Our personal encounter with the risen Christ will give a different quality to our lives. The difference between a Christian who merely encounters Jesus until Holy Week and one who encounters the resurrected Christ is vast. The Holy Week Christian is fearful, worried that he or she could be overcome or even condemned if he or she does not observe every religious law meticulously. These Christians are serious and sad; there is a heaviness about them and a lack of freedom. They consume themselves by making sure that others obey the law.

The Christians who encounter the risen Christ experience an empowering "fear and great joy." They live with energy and enthusiasm. They observe religious laws because they know that the laws lead to a deeper encounter with God; they are not simply avoiding being overcome or condemned. There is a lightness about them, and, wherever they go, people are filled with hope and feel encouraged by their joy and laughter.

Throughout my life, I have met many ministers and pastors. Many of them were good people, trying as best as they could. One man, however, stands out. Something was different about him. He was joyful and joked often. His hearty laughter often filled rooms and corridors. People from all walks of life came to him and, after their encounter with him, were filled with hope. He never seemed to tire and had an incredible courage and boldness. Even when he challenged people they never felt chastised; instead, they left encouraged. He was a man who truly loved those around him—no matter who they were, where they came from, or what they had done or failed to do. He was a man who had befriended the risen Christ.

- Who have been the courageous and bold witnesses to the risen Christ in your life? Pray for them today.
- How has your personal encounter with Jesus given your heart a different quality? How would you describe that quality?
- In what ways can you offer hope and encouragement to others, flowing from the hope and encouragement the risen Christ gives you?

Tuesday Easter Octave

Read Acts 2:26-41; Psalm 33;
John 20:11-18.

Excited new parents-to-be spend a lot of time thinking and talking about what they will name their child. Sometimes they look through books of names or their family tree to choose a name that is significant to them. Once parents have named a child, that name is for life. Names are important. They say something about who we are and where we come from. Names give us our identity. Names are personal. We are rightly offended when our names are spelled wrong or pronounced badly because they are intimate parts of us.

Notice the remarkable difference between Mary in the first and second part of the Gospel reading today. In the first part, the angels refer to her as "Woman." In the second part, Jesus calls her by name, and she immediately turns and responds. This is a warm and intimate moment, with Jesus taking the initiative to get Mary's attention. Mary recognizes Jesus because she knows his voice. She goes from weeping to proclaiming to the disciples, "I have seen the Lord" (John 20:18). Notice too how Mary's encounter with Jesus sets her free. The Mary we encounter in the first part of the Gospel is grieving. Distracted by her loss and grief, she cannot see what is really going on around her. She sees Jesus but does not recognize him. Only after she hears her name does she realize who he is. A change takes place. That change is symbolized in her recognition of Jesus. It is expressed in her response, "Rabbouni!" Mary is now free and sees more broadly than her loss and grief.

God does the same for us. God takes the initiative and calls us by name. God's invitation to us, like the invitation to Mary, is always personal. Sometimes we are so distracted by the many things we have to accomplish that our occupied minds miss the risen Jesus in our midst. Yet God never ceases, amid all that is going on in us and around us, to call us by name. When we respond, God opens our eyes and changes our perspective about ourselves and the world.

Moreover, after Jesus calls out to Mary and affirms her, he gives her a mission: "Go to my brothers and say to them, 'I am ascending to my Father and your Father'" (John 20:17). Our personal encounters with the Lord do not end with the encounter alone. When we encounter the Lord, we too are affirmed and given a mission by the Lord. Jesus sees the potential in us, like he saw in Mary, and sends us to be witnesses to his resurrection. We too are sent to tell others that we have "seen the Lord."

- Where did your name come from? Why or how was it chosen for you?
- When have you heard the risen Christ call your name?
- What affirmation and mission might the Lord be giving you?

Wednesday Easter Octave

Read Acts 3:1-10; Psalm 105;
Luke 24:13-35.

Doctor Brené Brown studies vulnerability, and she says in her 2010 talk at TedxHouston, "Vulnerability is the birthplace of innovation, creativity, and change." I thought of these words in relation to the scripture passages today. In Acts, Peter and John encounter a lame man who is vulnerable, and, in Luke, Jesus encounters two disciples who have vulnerable hearts. In both cases, vulnerability is the birthplace of innovation, creativity, and change as the people who meet Peter and John find new life and healing amid weakness.

The lame man asks Peter for alms. Peter does not give him alms but restores his legs so that he is mobile again. He walks and leaps and goes into the temple to praise God. Those around him are filled with "wonder and amazement" (Acts 3:10) at what has happened. Peter gives the man his mobility again "in the name of Jesus Christ of Nazareth" (Acts 3:6).

In Luke, we meet two disciples who feel defeated, let down, sad, and disillusioned. Perhaps they feel their lives have lost direction and that the things they had hoped for were only that: a vain hope. Their vulnerability is palpable. When Jesus walks with them, they do not recognize him. Their vulnerability blinds them. They commiserate about the tragic past and look toward a bleak future but are not able to live in the present. Jesus explains the scriptures to them, but they still don't know who he is. They are slow to believe. Upon reaching their destination, they invite this intriguing companion to stay with them. They recognize Jesus in the breaking of bread, and then he vanishes. Despite the lateness of the hour, the disciples head back to Jerusalem to tell others what has happened.

As we can see from these two stories, an encounter with the risen Christ gives us fresh perspectives and helps us see things anew. We ought not fear vulnerability but allow Jesus, our risen friend, to use our vulnerability to bring about "wonder and amazement." Jesus restores the immobile parts of us to mobility. He restores the hope of the disciples amid their fear and anxiety for what the future may hold. The risen Jesus heals physically but also emotionally and psychologically. He removes what blinds us and helps us see the past and future through the eyes of the present—and the truth of his resurrection. In and through the depth of our personal encounter with the risen Christ, the birthplace of innovation, creativity, and change emerges.

- Where do you feel vulnerable right now?
- How can you live in the truth of the risen Christ?
- What might be the birthplace of innovation, creativity, and change in your life right now?

Thursday Easter Octave

Read Acts 3:11-26; Psalm 8;
Luke 24:36-48.

Jesus, our friend, has immeasurable patience. In the Gospel scene today, he appears again to his disciples as they struggle to come to terms with his death and supposed resurrection. One of the most striking parts of this scene is how Jesus shows them his hands and his feet, and still they struggle to believe. He then asks them for a bite to eat to show them he is truly risen and alive. Notice how, even after eating the fish, he patiently explains to his disciples how what he told them before his death is being fulfilled.

We all struggle to be patient, and we live in an impatient world. The danger comes when we transfer our impatience onto God. Because we are impatient—or treated impatiently by others—we may begin to wonder if God is impatient like we are. Someone told me once that he always had thought God was impatient. Years before, a minister had been impatient with him and told him that God gets fed up with people when they just don't get it. This had a detrimental effect on his spiritual journey.

Peter, in the address we read today in Acts, gives a summary of salvation history. Starting with Abraham, Peter tries to explain how God, through time, can only be described as patient and has never given up on us. Today's psalm also alludes to God's never-ending patience with humanity. Notice, again, at the end of the passage in Luke, how Jesus, despite his disciples' unbelief, still tasks them to be "witnesses of these things" (Luke 24:48). God never gives up, no matter how much we struggle or how slow we are to respond.

Jesus invites us, his friends, to mirror that patience in our own lives. Our own experience of God's infinite patience—whether that be with our sinfulness or our slowness to respond or to believe—should encourage us to be the same for others. This is not always easy, especially when family members seek to annoy us, when people drive badly, or when situations confront us that are hard to accept. Yet these situations can reveal what we have learned about the depths of God's patience with us and can help us become true "witnesses" to God's work in the world. Let us live and treat others with the patience of God.

- In what ways has Jesus been infinitely patient with you?
- Describe a time when you wanted to give up on someone or a situation but strove to act with patience instead.
- Who in your life is in need of your loving patience?

Friday Easter Octave

Read Acts 4:1-12; Psalm 118;
John 21:1-14.

Today we reflect on one of the most powerful resurrection accounts in the Gospels: Jesus makes breakfast for his disciples. So many parts of this story are worth noting. Peter tells his companions that he is going fishing. Is he doing this out of economic necessity or as a sign that he is returning to his old way of life? Sometimes, when our lives have become uncertain, we go back to our old habits and ways of doing things. Unfortunately, Peter and the other disciples fish all night and catch nothing. Their efforts are futile. In this moment, they realize that going back to their old way of life is not an option. Their encounter and life with Jesus has changed them forever.

Then, Jesus appears on the scene and asks if they have caught anything. Jesus not only asks this question but also suggests that they cast their nets out on the right side of the boat. The disciples do so and catch so many fish that they cannot bring them all into the boat. Notice the difference: Alone, the disciples catch nothing; with Jesus, they find an abundance of fish. Haven't we experienced this in our own lives? What a difference between trying to do something alone and doing something with God.

When another disciple tells Peter that Jesus is the man who suggested they fish on the other side of the boat, Peter jumps out of the boat like an excited, uncontrollable child, leaving his poor companions to do all the work of bringing in the fish. Sometimes we need others—companions on the journey—to help us recognize the voice of the Lord.

Finally, this story, which begins with the disciples not sure of what to do and therefore resigning themselves to their old way of living—ends with an intimate meal with Jesus. The control has shifted to Jesus. He is the host, and, significantly, this is only the second meal he hosts. Jesus is normally the guest at meals. This meal gives us a picture of intimate fellowship. Jesus does not want to be our guest; the risen Christ wants to be our host. Can we, like the disciples, allow Jesus to be in control of the very direction our lives are taking?

- What are the "defaults" in your life when you feel uncertain or unsure?
- How have you seen a difference between the things you have tried to do alone and the things you have done with the Lord?
- The risen Christ wants to be your host. What hesitations do you have about handing over the control of the direction of your life to him?

Saturday Easter Octave

Read Acts 4:13-21; Psalm 118;
Mark 16:9-15.

Both New Testament texts today grapple with belief. In Acts, the rulers, elders, and scribes are concerned and can't believe what these "uneducated" and "ordinary men" are doing. In Mark, we read a summary of the disciples' unbelief. Cycles of belief and unbelief are part of our lives too. There are times when we feel an utter conviction and belief in the risen Christ. There are other times when we struggle to believe. This often happens when tragedy strikes. Our unbelief should not frighten us or make us feel guilty. Cycles of belief and unbelief are healthy. Admitting our weakness of faith or our doubt is an important part of our faith journey. One of the most dangerous fallacies we can hang on to is that we have to be perfect in faith and perfect in life in order for God to work in us and through us. This is not true. God always desires to work through us, even when our faith might seem thin or frail.

Notice what happens at the end of the passage in Mark. Even though Jesus chastises the disciples for not believing after his many efforts to get through to them, he does not stop there. He tells the disciples, "Go into all the world and proclaim the good news to the whole creation" (Mark 16:15). Even the disciples' dodgy faith is not enough to stop Jesus. Our unbelief does not stop God.

Contrast the passage from Mark to the passage in Acts. Unbelief has given way to belief. We meet a bold Peter and a courageous John. Being charged not to speak about Jesus by the civil authorities has no effect on them. Notice the bold answer they give the authorities. They are not worried about what they think; they will speak—they tell them—about what they have seen and heard. No threat can stop Peter and John from proclaiming the good news of the risen Christ.

Jesus gives us a task like that of his disciples. We are to share the truth of Jesus' resurrection with the world. In the days after Easter, we are invited to move from the introspection of Lent to the proclamation of the good news. It is in the midst of proclaiming the gospel that we will come to see our own belief deepen. Are we ready to take on the challenge that will lead us to a deeper faith and offer a new perspective?

- Where have you seen the cycle of belief and unbelief in your life?
- When has your unbelief failed to stop Jesus from working through you?
- In the days and weeks to come, how will you "Go into all the world and proclaim the good news to the whole creation"?

Second Sunday of Easter

Read Acts 5:12-16; Psalm 118; Revelation 1:9-13, 17-19; John 20:19-31.

Today's Gospel reading contains a powerful lesson: No person, situation, or place is beyond God's reach. God, in Jesus, can enter where none of us can go. The disciples are afraid. Their friend Jesus, in whom they have placed much hope, was killed in front of their eyes. Then, they hear reports that he is risen. They think that because they are associated with Jesus, they could be the target of the authorities. They lock themselves in a house in fear. Jesus effortlessly comes to them and says, "Peace be with you" (John 20:19). Jesus not only offers them peace but also tasks them with forgiving the sins of people. A few days later, Jesus again breaks through their walls to say, "Peace be with you" (John 20:26). He shows Thomas his hands and his side. Thomas could not believe the account given to him by his companions, and Jesus, knowing Thomas's struggle, breaks through his wall of unbelief.

In the text from Acts, the writer tells us how God, through the apostles, can break down the barriers of sickness and unclean spirits, reaching out to people no matter who they are, where they have come from, or what they have done. Nothing is beyond God's reach. God, in Jesus, can reach beyond our human imagining into places and situations that we can't. Jesus does not build walls but moves through walls. Jesus reads hearts and is able to enter places where we do not want to go or cannot go.

How fitting that our reflections end on this Sunday, which is also called Divine Mercy Sunday. Divine mercy knows no bounds. We accept God's divine mercy in our willingness to be open to God's many possibilities and in our ability to hold those opportunities open for others. When we help others know and feel that they are included, welcomed, loved, and cherished for who they are, we are showing others divine mercy. Every day presents us with opportunities at home, work, or even in our supermarkets to reach out to others in loving service.

The depth of our friendship with Jesus will determine if we have a growing faith of consolation or a shrinking faith of desolation; a faith with its foot on the gas or a faith with its foot on the brakes; a Christian life that is joyful and can recognize the essence of the gospel or a Christian life of depletion and grim duty. John tells us, at the end of the Gospel reading, that believing in Jesus will bring us life in his name. It is now our task to live that life and offer life to others.

- When have you seen God's reach extended to any person, situation, or place?
- When have you, in seemingly impossible situations, heard Jesus say, "Peace be with you"?
- How can you be a vessel of God's boundless mercy for others?

ABOUT THE AUTHORS

Anthony Egan is a Jesuit priest on the staff of the Jesuit Institute. He does theological and political analysis. He also teaches part-time at the Steve Biko Centre for Bioethics at the University of the Witwatersrand and assists at the chaplaincy to university students. He has been published extensively in books and journals around the world and is well known for his acute commentary on theological and social issues in South Africa.

Trevor Hudson is a Methodist minister. He assists in teaching the Jesuit Institute's Spiritual Directors Training and Spiritual Exercises Training. He is based at Northfields Methodist in Benoni, South Africa, but preaches and teaches all over the country and internationally. Trevor is sought after as a spiritual director. He is the author of thirteen books, including several from Upper Room Books.

Russell Pollitt is a Jesuit priest and currently director of the Jesuit Institute South Africa. He does commentary and analysis on the Catholic Church and the sociopolitical situation in South Africa. He writes for South Africa's online newspaper, *Daily Maverick*. He is interested in media and communications and how technology affects spirituality.